SIMPLY

PAPER
CUTTING

* * * * * * * * * * * * *

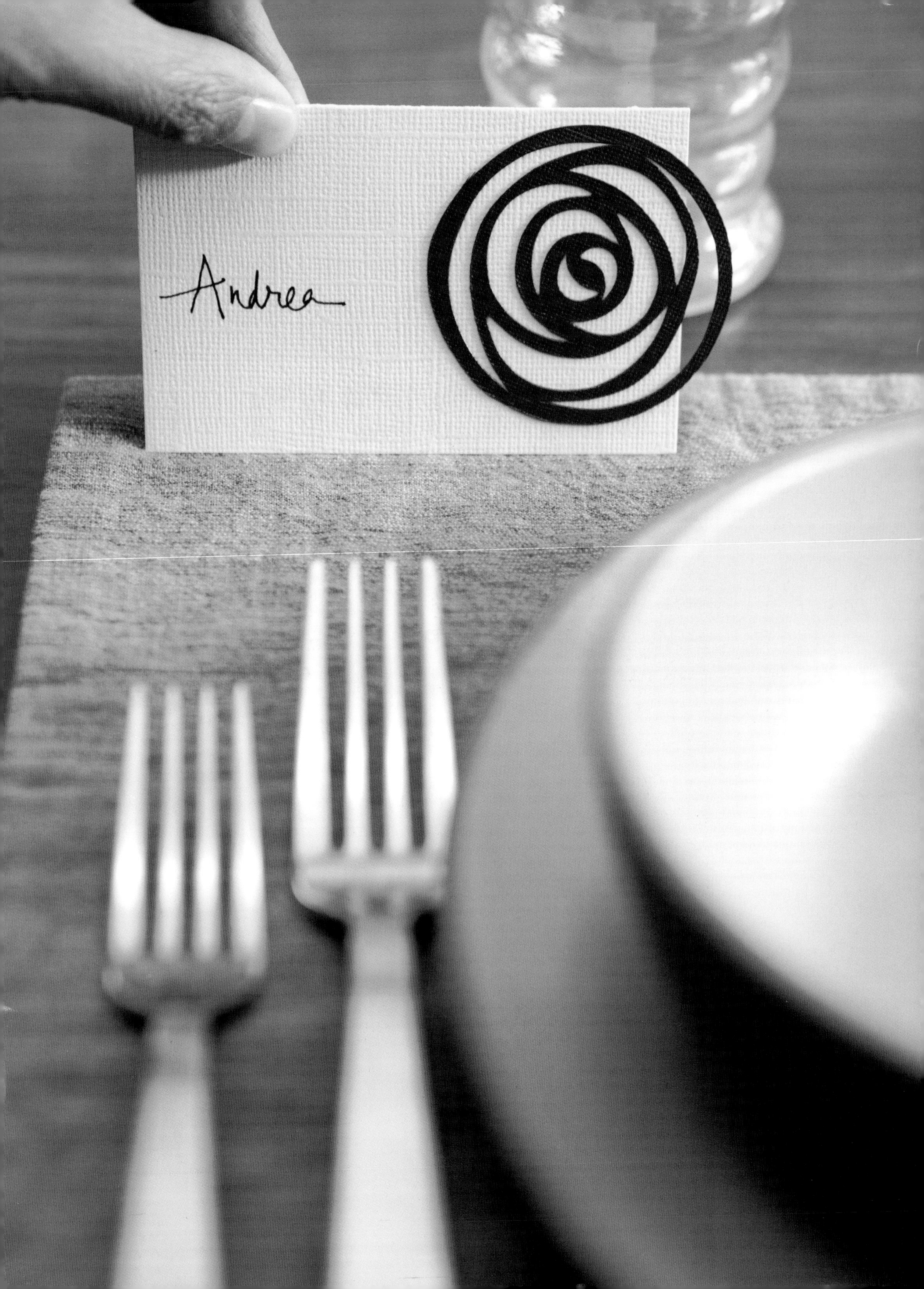
Andrea

SIMPLY
PAPER
CUTTING

* * * * * * * * * * * * * *

HAND-CUT PAPER PROJECTS
FOR HOME DÉCOR, STATIONERY & GIFTS

anna bondoc

Design Originals

an Imprint of Fox Chapel Publishing
www.d-originals.com

"A Cut Above"
Place Cards, page 50
PHOTO BY LISA FRANCHOT.

DEDICATION:

For Matthew and Claire, whose love makes a well-designed life possible.

ACKNOWLEDGMENTS

Photography:
Cover and glamour photography: Lisa Franchot
Step-by-step photography: Vanessa Trice Peter
Pre-shoot planning and training: Roxanne Davis

With heartfelt gratitude to:
Vanessa Trice Peter: for making business a pleasure and putting all great things within reach.
Fox Chapel Publishing: with special thanks to Peg Couch, Kerri Landis, Judith McCabe, and Traci Niese for their enthusiastic, prudent guidance.
Joann Davis: for sharing an artful, lovely home that showed my work in its best light.

Company credits: Anna Bondoc LLC
Creative Director/Founder: Anna Bondoc
CEO/Founder: Vanessa Trice Peter
Intellectual Property attorneys: Milord & Associates, P.C.
Junior design assistants: Claire Sand, Norah Peter

Anna Bondoc links:
Website: *annabondoc.com*
Facebook: *facebook.com/annabondocdesigns*
Twitter: *twitter.com/annabondoc*
Pinterest: *pinterest.com/annabondoc*
Etsy: *etsy.com/shop/annabondocdesigns*

For more information on Anna Bondoc, ANNA BONDOC® fine art, stationery, and gifts, contact *info@annabondoc.com*.

For more information on licensing ANNA BONDOC® designs, contact *info@annabondoc.com* or intellectual property counsel at *milordlaw.com*.

ISBN 978-1-57421-418-5

© 2012 by Anna Bondoc and Design Originals, www.d-originals.com, 800-457-9112, 1970 Broad Street, East Petersburg, PA 17520.

Library of Congress Cataloging-in-Publication Data

Bondoc, Anna (Artisan)
 Simply paper cutting : hand-cut paper projects for home decor, stationery and gifts / Anna Bondoc. -- First [edition].
\(pages cm
 Includes index.
  ISBN 978-1-57421-418-5 (pbk.)
 1. Paper work--Patterns. I. Title.
TT870.B588 2012
 745.54--dc23
                         2012014074

Printed in China
First Printing

About Me

I am an artist, designer, teacher, writer, and avid home cook.

I developed my unique paper cutting technique in 2005 shortly after I became a new mother and was looking for a way to continue printmaking without toxic paints and solvents. Experimenting with a craft knife and colored cardstock, I cut patterns into paper, adding additional paper layers and cuts as I went. This yielded tactile, intricate graphic patterns, which I sold as a collection of handmade cards to Soolip and Gump's. I used the funds from that and a private commission to rent my first studio. Friend and business dynamo Vanessa Trice Peter and I started scheming, and soon afterward we launched Anna Bondoc Designs in 2010.

Much of my inspiration comes from a bone-deep passion for Japanese and Scandinavian design and home furnishings. I gravitate toward artists and artistic periods filled with bold, biomorphic shapes in striking compositions and saturated colors. For creative recharge, I turn to the works of Eva Zeisel, Isamu Noguchi, Sam Maloof, and Marimekko, as well as the Arts & Crafts, German Expressionist, Wiener Werkstatte, and Mid-Century Modern movements.

I am also a passionate teacher. Before 2005, I taught middle and high school English and became a Founding Parent and Volunteer Teacher at the Larchmont Charter West Hollywood School in 2007. I enjoy designing visual and language arts curricula that empower students with skills needed to unleash their self-expression. I hope this passion is reflected in the book you hold in your hands.

My writing and designs have also appeared in *Traditional Home Magazine*; *Cloth, Paper, Scissors*; *Stitch*; *Better Homes and Gardens' Make It Yourself Magazine*; and in various blogs, including *Daily Candy* and *Apartment Therapy*.

I live in Los Angeles with my husband, daughter, and oh-so-gentle pit bull and revel in the sun, canyon hikes, access to mind-boggling produce, swimming, public tennis courts, and a culturally sophisticated and diverse urban environment.

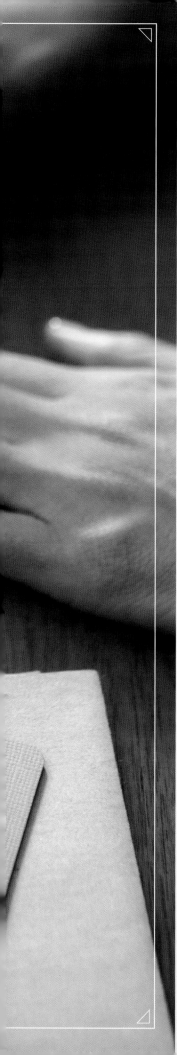

Contents

Gift Card Holder, page 126
PHOTO BY LISA FRANCHOT.

How To Use This Book

Begin with the Basic Techniques

I invite you to learn from my seven years of hard-won paper-cutting techniques to help you bypass frustration. The skills aren't particularly difficult, but they are unique to my process. The Basic Techniques tutorials (pp. 18–35) let you practice every single skill required to complete any of the 15 projects in this book, and will give your hands "muscle memory" of the movements.

Learn to Love Your Master Stencils

Each project requires that you create a master stencil, which involves transferring my hand-drawn black-and-white designs from this book to cardstock so you can retain templates to easily stencil and cut each paper layer. Cutting a master stencil is both a wonderful way to warm-up and, more important, a kind of record of your design so you can easily make multiple journals, cards, or bunting later on.

All the patterns in this book are colored by what level they are. This way, you can tell at a glance which pattern goes with which layer. A handy thumbnail-size image in the corner of all the pattern pages also shows how the patterns will look when stacked together. Green is the top (first) layer, light purple is the bottom (second) layer, and orange is used for any pieces placed on top. Note that some of the pieces placed on top don't have a complete pattern to copy and use as a template, but instead show the illustration of one shape for you to reference and apply where needed—these are shaded yellow.

Recycle by Design

Because the knife creates shapes by *subtracting* them from paper, you will pile up little delicate cutaway shapes on the side of your cutting mat. Those shapes will call out to you, "Create something else with me!" At the end of many project chapters, "You May Also Try" sidebars suggest easy ways to use those cutaways to create even more designs.

Work Your Way Up

Each project is ranked by difficulty, ranging from Beginner to Advanced—keep a lookout for the icon in the upper left of each project start page. Stick to beginner rankings at first, and work your way up until you've made everything!

Itching to Start?

Safety first!

Read the safety tips (pg. 17) to alleviate any anxiety you may have about using a knife as your design tool.

Go as slowly as you need to.

Paper cutting requires rigorous arm movements and intense concentration. Get up and stretch as often as needed between cuts to keep your cutting skills fresh and precise.

Forget perfectionism.

The pieces should look handmade. People like to see that a human hand made their gift. Paper is a relatively inexpensive, plentiful medium. At worst, you can get a fresh sheet of paper or start again.

BASIC TECHNIQUES IN A NUTSHELL

- Move the entire cutting arm from shoulder to fingertips.
- Use your non-cutting hand to turn the paper.
- Align your paper along the mat's grid lines when measuring.
- Use as little glue as possible.
- Burnish as you adhere each paper layer.
- Erase in one direction only in a dab-and-pull motion.

Dessert Stencils, page 38

Cupcake Toppers, page 44

Place Cards, page 50

Cake Wrap, page 56

Journal Set, page 64

Gift Box Trio, page 70

Holiday Ornaments,
page 78

Decorative Frame,
page 86

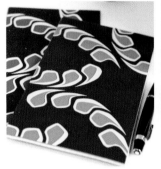

Kids' Wall Art, page 94

Flower Triptych,
page 102

Arts & Crafts Bunting,
page 106

Happy Hour Gift Tag,
page 114

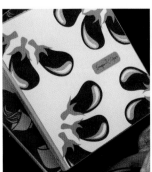

Recipe Binder, page 120

Gift Card Set, page 126

Stationery Set, page 132

ALL PHOTOS ON THIS PAGE BY LISA FRANCHOT.

Introduction: Life in Layers

Like most people who first encounter my work, chances are you saw the cover of this book and thought the cake skirt was screen printed, collaged, or letter pressed. I always invite people to come closer to touch my designs to see their surprised smiles as they realize they're touching layered, cut paper. There's just something magical about paper cuts—remember feeling elated as a kid the moment you unfolded a paper snowflake?

In plainest words, my designs are layers of cardstock that have been hand cut and glued to form intricate patterns. I've tried fancier phrases like "paper cuts," "reverse collages," "paper silk screening," and "layered patterns," but really, it's best to see them in person to appreciate them. The good news is that by using the techniques in this book you can make, see, and touch 15-plus layered paper designs—either for yourself or others.

How I Discovered My Technique

It would sound snazzy to say I developed my design process by studying the rich history of paper cutting techniques from China, Japan, Poland, and Mexico. But the truth is that a combination of new motherhood, limited space, and a printmaking background led me to my unique method of paper cutting.

The year my daughter was born, I tried making art while she napped. I needed a process that didn't require lengthy drying time, clean up, or toxic chemicals. This eliminated my first loves, printmaking and silk screening. I had always collected specialty papers, so I begin tinkering with collage, working at my small desk with a cutting mat, craft knife, and glue. Then one day, while cutting a row of petal shapes into a sheet of brown cardstock, I got up to feed the baby and returned to find the brown sheet with cutouts resting atop a red one. The see-through effect enchanted me: the petal shapes became windows to the red paper below. I glued brown to red, cut shapes inside the red paper, and then glued a yellow layer beneath that. I continued cutting and gluing in a kind of archaeological dig, designing and cutting downward.

This process mimicked the linoleum block printing I fell in love with in high school art class: each graphic element split into separate color layers, yet coming together into a single bold composition. The bonus was that gluing paper layers was fast and eliminated the need for a printing press or mixing inks. Using my hands and cutting the same motif repeatedly brought a soothing predictability—a needed respite from the unpredictable trials of new motherhood!

Cupcake Toppers, page 44
PHOTO BY LISA FRANCHOT.

I refined my process for several months, learning to swivel my wrist with more skill to make more precise cuts. I tested adhesives, pencils, and blades. A pivotal moment was stumbling on gorgeous textured scrapbooking cardstock in a range of rich, saturated hues that rivaled the best acrylic paints and oil pastels. This allowed me to develop sophisticated color ways. My designs soared, and I sold my first collection of greeting cards to high-end stationery stores. Soon after, I landed my first fine art commission and used the funds to rent studio space—a lifelong dream of mine. In the summer of 2010, with my business partner, Vanessa, I launched a design studio.

Worth Repeating

Though I've been inspired by many wonderful paper craft books, I wanted my own to make my idiosyncratic technique accessible to everyone, including absolute beginners. I recall a talented crochet artist asking if I could teach her paper cutting. Assuming it would be easy for her, I watched her struggle to make even a basic straight cut. I had taken for granted that holding a craft knife isn't just like drawing, but rather requires a combination of strength and finesse, and gross and fine motor skills. If I were to teach my craft, I'd need to cover the basics: how to position one's hands to make every type of paper cut, make a stencil, measure paper with pinpoint accuracy, and even apply glue.

Though you may want to dive right into making a journal or gift card holder, I encourage you to explore my Basic Techniques tutorials (pp. 18–35), including: cutting different kinds of lines, gluing neatly, aligning and measuring precisely, even erasing to avoid tearing. Take the time to try your skills on scrap paper first when the stakes are low, and then, by all means, dive right in and make some beautiful paper art!

Learn the Rules to Break Them

This craft takes a precise person who enjoys cutting patterns into paper with a knife. But my technique also appeals to artists, designers, and wildly inventive people, too. I intended this book for anyone who wants to master cutting skills, and then break free to design his/her own paper craft projects. Who knows how you might upcycle boxes and journals, or take the cutaway scraps from one of my book's projects and compose an entirely different pattern?

With that, I invite you to dig into this book, learn my techniques, and branch out. I look forward to getting photos of the designs you've devised. Drop me a line at anna@annabondoc.com.

Slice on, paper crafters!

Getting Started

* * * * * * * * * * * * * * * * *

In this chapter, get the ins and outs of basic tools and materials

and safety tips, then roll up your sleeves for hands-on tutorials

to practice all the techniques you'll need to make layered

paper cuts.

Tools and Materials

Many paper craft books encourage you to explore a variety of tools and papers, but the spirit of my technique is to keep tools and materials to a minimum, saving complexity for the paper patterns. You can complete the projects in this book with the following essentials.

Cardstock

To capture the subtle beauty of layered paper, choose monochromatic paper that's thick enough to throw slight shadows and to withstand sketching, cutting, erasing, and gluing. Eighty-pound cardstock is best, especially because it's thick enough for use as stencils. Anything higher than 90-pound will likely be too thick to cut. For these projects, 12" x 12" (305 x 305mm) scrapbook sheets are excellent as they are large enough to cover the surface areas of journals, frames, and gift boxes. With careful planning, you can glean multiple projects from a single sheet.

I first developed my cut-layer-cut-again technique using Bazzill Basics monochromatic cardstock. Bazzill's range of colors is astounding, plus the textured finishes are a tactile treat. There are other 80-pound scrapbooking paper brands available online or at scrapbooking stores (see p. 142 for sources). Be sure they are acid-free so that your wall art and keepsake gifts last. Though the color choices are more limited, you might also experiment with Canson paper, watercolor paper, and Bristol paper, which are available at art and craft stores and websites.

Practice paper

Try keeping recycled report covers, kraft paper, or regular printer paper on hand for warm-up and practicing cutting techniques.

Craft knife

I've come to think of my knife as a drawing tool that *subtracts* shapes from paper rather than adding them. Invest in an ergonomic rubber-grip craft knife, such as X-ACTO's X2000 with a rubberized barrel and safety cap (shown in this book). It's more economical to purchase a box of 100 blades, size #11, as you will need to change them frequently. (See Basic Techniques and the Safety sidebar on p. 17 for more on using craft knives to full advantage.) The knife is well known as a precision blade that cuts and trims, but I also use it to pick up and position even the tiniest pieces, to score paper, and even to scrape away dried glue. **Author's note:** After writing this book, I started using the X-ACTO Z blade. It has a distinctive gold edge to distinguish it from the

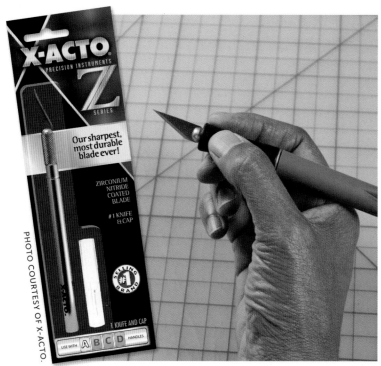

PHOTO COURTESY OF X-ACTO.

Craft knife as drawing tool. The X-ACTO Z blade (left) is my craft knife of choice. An ergonomic rubber-grip craft knife, such as the X-ACTO X2000 (right) model with a rubberized barrel and safety cap, is also a great craft knife choice.

normal blade. I only use this blade now. The blades are very sharp and the tips don't break off. Highly recommended!

Cutting mat

The self-healing cutting mat is essential to paper craft art. It absorbs the blade's impact, protecting work surfaces and preventing the blade from dulling quickly. The magical mat surface reseals as you cut rather than creating ridges that would eventually render a bumpy and unsafe surface. I've come to appreciate the way the mat provides a cushioned feeling, which gives me a sense of the speed and fluidity of my cuts. I use the 24" x 36" (610 x 915mm) reversible Alvin mat, which makes cutting down oversized sheets easier and can be flipped over after one side has worn out. If space is limited or you prefer a smaller mat, try an 18" x 24" (460 x 610mm) model.

Your mat is also a critical measuring tool. The best mats feature measurements on four sides, making it easy to measure precisely in conjunction with your ruler. Use the all-over grid to align paper at right angles so that your sheets are accurately and consistently squared off.

Metal straightedge ruler

I recommend an 18" (150mm) metal ruler with cork backing. You'll be trimming 12" x 12" (305 x 305mm) sheets, so the ruler must be long enough to hang over and brace the entire sheet at once. Cork backing prevents the ruler from slipping while you cut. (In a pinch, apply masking tape to the back side.) Avoid plastic rulers, because blades will nick or even shear the ruler's edges. Seek out a ruler with rounded edges because the sharp metal corners can scratch.

Liquid adhesive

My glue of choice is Tombow Mono-Multi Adhesive. It's fast drying, permanent, and acid-free, yet also forgiving. It's relatively easy to reposition paper if you act quickly before the glue has a chance to set. A little goes a long way, too. Apply it using the kindergarten teacher's maxim, "Dot, dot, not a lot," and the paper will adhere firmly without unsightly buckling or bubbling. The bottle has two applicator tips: a tiny one for narrow spaces and a wider end for larger areas. Dried glue spots are removed easily with an adhesive pick-up square.

Printing baren

After you glue one paper layer to another, burnish or buff them together with a printing baren to evenly set and distribute the glue, especially on corners. I first used a baren in linoleum block printing class. This lightweight disk with a handle is used to rub paper onto an inked block to transfer the ink. Barens are available in the printmaking section of most general art supply stores or online. Though you could use the heel of your hand, the natural oils, liquid, glue, or pencil lead on your hands can transfer to your design. In a pinch, tuck your hand into a clean oven mitt or piece of fabric to smooth and flatten the paper layers.

tip: SELF-HEALING MAT LONGEVITY

To ensure your mat's long life, store it flat and out of direct sunlight, and rotate it regularly. Wipe the surface to remove dried glue and debris.

Pencils

Keep pencils on hand to sketch designs, stencil, plot out measurement lines, and mark the position of motifs before you glue them. I prefer soft lead pencils in the B range (my favorite is 2B or 3B). Soft lead is darker and easier to see as you cut, and when used with a light hand, erases more readily than the harder H pencils, which can dig lines into the cardstock.

Adhesive pick-up square

Though artists may no longer use rubber cement that often, adhesive pick-up squares (often called rubber cement erasers) are still around. I use them almost exclusively for my projects because they simultaneously remove pencil sketch marks and excess dried glue without leaving eraser bits behind. They tend to darken with use, but it's easy enough to pick off the dried glue that collects on the corners. I sometimes cut erasers into triangles, creating more corners, which reach nooks and crannies of layered paper designs. A good alternative is the Magic Rub eraser, but use an eraser brush to remove eraser bits.

Optional tools and materials

The following tools and materials are helpful to have on hand, but not necessary.

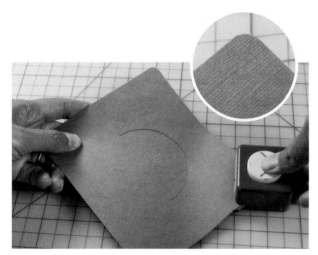

The handy corner rounder. Invest in an inexpensive corner rounder to lend paper crafts finished, modern chic.

Re-sealable bags: As you cut out shapes, store the ones you like most in small re-sealable polypropylene bags that beads or gift cards are packaged in. (Uline sells them in bulk.) Keep the bags in a box, then "upcycle" these scraps in a myriad of creative ways. I collage the shapes into patterns to decorate blank note cards and glue them as embellishments on gift boxes and gift tags, for example.

Low-tack masking tape: Keep a roll of low-tack tape (¾" or 19mm width is fine) to position paper temporarily. Tape down master stencils to prevent them from sliding or secure cardstock on the cutting mat to prevent it from coming out of alignment on the cutting mat as you measure. Be sure to remove the tape slowly to prevent ripping.

Paper cutter: Perhaps you decide to create in larger quantities, say for weddings or holidays. A rotary paper cutter can significantly speed up the process by measuring and trimming cards, journal covers, place cards, or other square or rectangle shapes. When I was a child, paper cutters were scary, scythe-like things, but today's cutters by Elmer's, Fiskars, CARL, and others have locking bars that hold down your paper firmly as you slide the protected rotary blade along a guide bar. Some models include scoring and perforating blades.

Corner rounder: I stumbled on this humble little cutting tool at an office supply store. I use it to give paper crafts a finished, modern chic. I've tried several but keep returning to the CARL Corner Rounding Punch CP-6A, an inexpensive model that cuts small radius corners easily. Simply insert paper until it rests flush against the rounder's 90-degree corner and depress the button completely until you hear a solid thunk. Punch one paper layer at a time (two at most), re-punching if necessary each time you glue an additional layer. The corner punch rarely punches through three or more layers of cardstock.

Paper sealants and coating: Consider using a sealant to protect projects such as the journal (p. 64) or picture frame (p. 86). Aerosol acrylic sealant sprays such as Krylon's UV-Resistant Clear Acrylic Coating can be applied quickly. Read manufacturers' labels closely and apply in a well-aerated space. Spray projects propped up at an angle (rather than flat) because the sealant tends to pool and create dark spots.

In my experience, the spray can turn paper a slightly darker shade once applied. If you have patience (and prefer a water-based, non-aerosol product), try Mod Podge for Paper applied with a foam brush. Apply in very thin coats and allow to dry thoroughly between coats. The multiple paper layers can buckle with overly thick application.

SAFETY

Here are a few pointers for avoiding accidents when cutting paper.

Change blades often: *Sharp = safe* and *dull = dangerous*. Sharp blades dig firmly into paper while dull blades skid on the paper's surface. You'll feel when a blade becomes dull and doesn't catch as firmly into the paper; change it immediately. And when trimming through multiple layers, always begin with a fresh blade.

Keep craft knives in a contained space: Knives can roll off of your table or disappear under a piece of paper only to be found by your fingertip. Either secure the safety cap, or in the midst of a project, place your knife inside a canister or an art box. I keep mine in an artist's bin with dividers, with blades facing the same direction. The bin has removable dividers that allow me to customize interior storage space to house my knives, erasers, glue, pencils, and sharpeners in one spot. (See Resources, p. 142)

Work in the middle of your table and mat: I cut at least 8" (205mm) from the table edge, putting me squarely in the middle of my mat, clear of my torso and legs. Unless you are cutting north to south, try to cut at a slight angle to the left or right of your torso. If cutting north to south, position your body just to the left or right of the ruler.

Brush debris from your mat: Before you cut, sweep the mat area each time you lay down a fresh sheet of paper. Even small bits of eraser, glue, or paper cuttings may find their way beneath the cardstock, creating little speed bumps that throw off your cuts.

Install proper lighting: Your work desk should be well lit. A basic gooseneck lamp or artist's lamp clamped over the edge of your desk with soft white bulb is fine. I invested in a lamp that mimics daylight to ease eye strain and ensure I have a clear view of both pencil guide lines and knife position at all times. (See Resources, p. 142, for artist lamps.)

Take breaks: These projects require both sharp eyes and strong hands. Eyes and hands are muscles that experience fatigue, and accidents happen when you are both tired and/or distracted. Better to walk away from a project and relax your eyes and hands than to stay and make dangerous mistakes.

Dispose blades in a container: Never throw old blades in the garbage—they are still sharp enough to hurt whoever takes out the bag. I keep an old coffee can with a lid that I throw used blades into—it has literally taken me years of paper cutting to fill! If/when you fill the can, cover it and toss it into the recycling bin.

Basic Techniques & Tutorials

Whether you're a beginner or experienced craft knife handler, these exercises will boost your confidence before you dive into the projects. Don't worry if you make jagged or inaccurate cuts for a little while. Keep practicing with scrap cardstock or printer paper. Like any art form, it takes time to get a feel for the tools and materials.

TOOLS AND MATERIALS

Gather these materials and tools for these tutorials:

- Craft knife, such as X-ACTO, with rubber grip
- Blades, such as #11 X-ACTO blades
- Self-healing cutting mat
- Liquid adhesive for paper
- 18" (460mm) metal ruler

- Adhesive pick-up square
- Low-tack masking tape or stencil tape
- B series pencil (2B or 3B)
- ¼" (6mm)-radius corner rounder

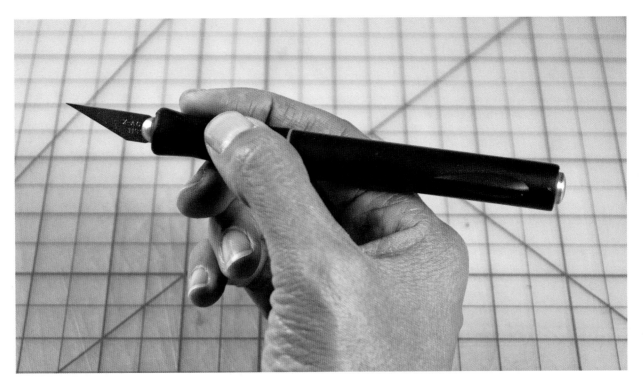

Make friends with your knife. Hold the knife as you would a pencil to feel where your fingers are most comfortable.

Technique 1:
Get comfortable with your craft knife

Make friends with your craft knife. First, hold it as you would a pencil to feel where your fingers are most comfortable. Notice how the upper barrel (above the metal ring) twists to hold or release the blade from its clamp. Because it's safest to work with a sharp blade, it's important to get comfortable replacing it.

Practice This: Replace the Knife Blade

Grasp the knife's base with one hand and with the other, turn the top of the barrel *counterclockwise* to loosen the blade clamp. Carefully pinch the blade's dull side and pull up slowly to remove it and dispose of it in a can. Pick up a new blade by its dull side and insert it into the knife slit, pushing down as far as it will go. Rotate the barrel top *clockwise* while continuing to push the blade downward to lock the blade in place. Now you're ready to cut.

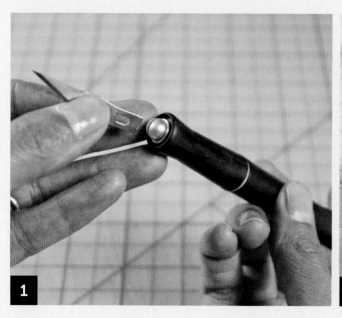
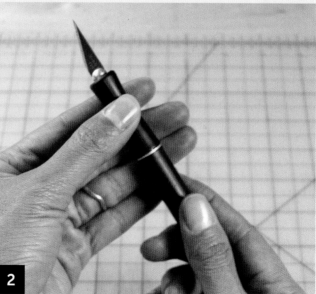

Technique 2:
Position both hands properly

You'll hold a craft knife as you would a pencil, but there is a critical difference: while writing with a pencil, the side of your hand from fingertip to wrist rests atop the paper as you draw. Cutting and drawing with a knife, however, requires a wider range of motion, so the only part of your cutting hand that should remain on the mat is from *pinky tip to the first knuckle*. This way, the pinky becomes a pivot point, allowing your thumb, fore-, and middle fingers to move the knife with more

force and range. You may even need to push up onto the pinky tip while negotiating tighter curves.

Your non-cutting hand is active, too. Use it to either hold the cardstock steady or rotate the paper as you cut. Keep your fingertips cupped (rather than flat) as a piano player holds her hands on the keys so that the non-cutting hand can readily angle the paper to help you reach a cut. Plus, you'll be less tempted to swivel your neck.

Use both hands. You need both hands to make a good cut. Keep the non-knife hand cupped and ready to steady or turn the paper.

safety tip: HAND POSITION

Keep your non-cutting hand north and west (if right-handed) or east (if left-handed) of the knife's cutting path. Always cut in the middle of your table or desk, leaving a good 8" (205mm) between your work and your torso and lap.

Practice This: Use Both Hands in Tandem

Sketch a half circle (see illustration) about the diameter of a teacup on a piece of paper and lay it on the cutting mat. Hold your craft knife as described on page 20, resting your non-cutting hand to the north of the semicircle with fingertips cupped. With your cutting hand resting on the first pinky knuckle only, gently slide the knife tip along the arc and along the curve. Use the non-cutting hand to slightly rotate the paper as you go. Notice how resting your cutting hand on its pinky tip frees your wrist to move smoothly around the semi-circle.

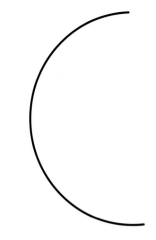

Basic Technique 2: Semicircle

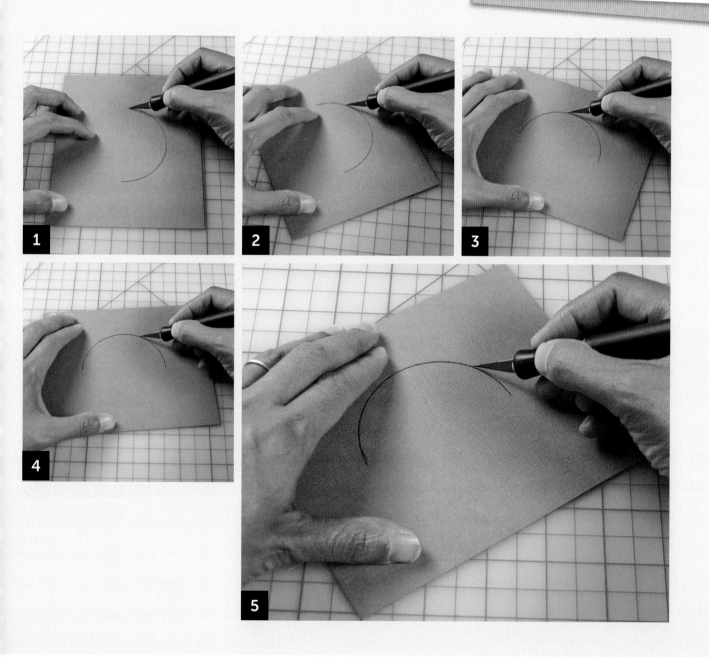

Technique 3:
Push down and pull through

When I first started designing with a knife, I used just my fingers and wrist to move the knife. I soon discovered more success—and less frustration—if I used the strength of my entire arm. To make clean cuts, move the entire arm from shoulder to fingertips to exert steady, firm pressure on the knife as you pull. With every cut, push the blade down into the mat while simultaneously pulling the knife through a stenciled line. It may help to say to yourself, "Push down and pull through."

Practice This: Cut Parallel Lines

Lay a piece of cardstock about 5" x 5" (130 x 130mm) on your mat. Sketch five to six parallel lines about 2" (50mm) long as seen in the illustration. Insert the blade tip at the top of a line and push the blade down until you feel it make contact with the mat. Working from the *shoulder*, pull the knife down and toward you through the sketched line, applying even, direct pressure as you go. Your elbow should move down and toward your torso as you do this. Repeat this full-arm motion for each line. Lift the paper up to the light to see if you applied enough pressure to cut cleanly through the paper.

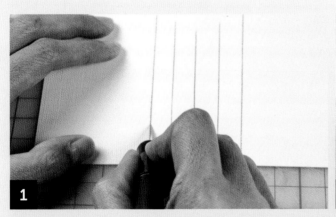

tip: SMUDGE PROTECTOR

Trim a small piece of scrap cardstock about 3" x 5" (75 x 130mm) to tuck beneath your non-cutting hand. This will prevent you from transferring your fingers' natural oils onto the paper surfaces, particularly during warmer weather.

Technique 4:
Pivot your wrist

Now, try cutting zigzags and curves. This motion combines Techniques 2 and 3, plus wrist pivoting with both hands. Remember to work from the shoulder and upper arm, pushing down and through.

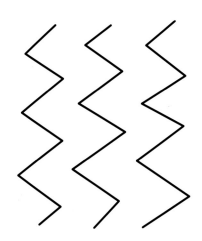

Basic Technique 4: Jagged Lines

Practice This: Cut Jagged Lines

Sketch zigzag lines like those in the illustration on scrap cardstock. Cut each zig and zag from top to bottom. Notice how you must pick up your knife at each corner of the zigzag and pivot your cutting hand to the right and left. Keep your neck steady, using your non-cutting hand to angle and pivot the paper to negotiate the cuts.

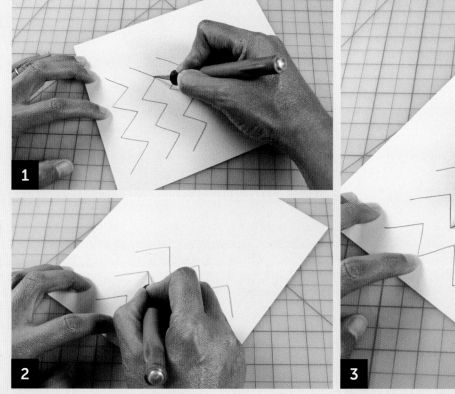

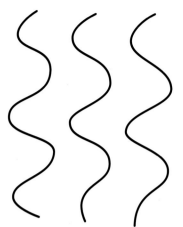

Basic Technique 4: Curvy Lines

Practice This: Cut Curvy Lines

Now sketch wavy lines like those in the illustration. Guide your knife along the curves *without* removing the blade tip from the paper, if possible. Pivot elbow and wrist to swivel the blade as you negotiate the curves. Remember to "push down, pull through," with the entire arm. Use your non-cutting hand to turn the paper to help.

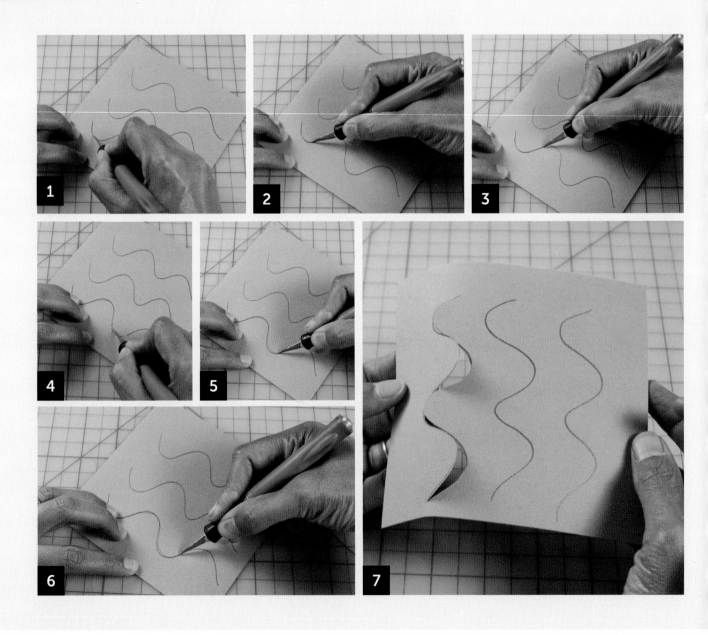

Technique 5:
Cut clean corners

As you learned while cutting zigzags in Technique 4, sharp corners require you to lift your knife from the cardstock to reposition the blade tip. If the zig and zag don't meet up at the corner, the paper will hang by a divot when you try to remove the shape. Try this "cross over" technique to prevent or remedy that problem.

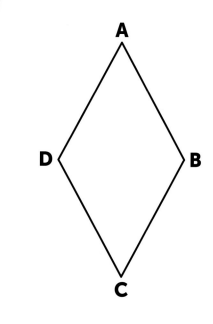

Basic Technique 5: Diamond

Practice This: Make Clean Cuts at Corners

Sketch a diamond with points A, B, C, and D as shown in the illustration. Cut line AB. Just before you cut line BC, reposition the blade tip so it forms a tiny X with line AB. Press down on the knife blade and cut line BC. Continue creating tiny X's at each corner to ensure the entire shape detaches cleanly from the cardstock.

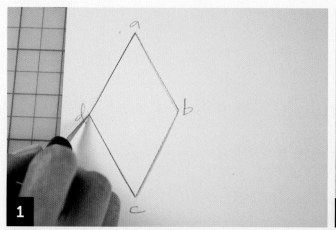

1

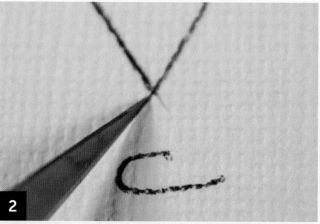

2

tip: REMOVING SOLID SHAPES

To remove a solid shape, push your blade into its center and gently lift it out. If the shape resists, locate the spot(s) where the paper remains attached. Reposition your blade in the cutting path ¼" (6mm) before the stuck spot; now you have a "running start" to re-cut the attachment.

Technique 6:
Measure and trim precise rectangles

Many projects ask you to trim rectangles to size. If a rectangle's opposite sides aren't aligned and parallel, or its corners don't line up at right angles, your design will be skewed. Happily, you can use your cutting mat and ruler in tandem to measure with great accuracy. Practice aligning your paper and sliding the knife blade along the metal ruler at the correct angle.

Practice This: Cut Two Identical Rectangles

1 **Place the paper.** The goal here is to cut two rectangles of 4" x 6" (100 x 150mm) so that they can be glued perfectly flush with each other. Place a 12" x 12" (305 x 305mm) cardstock sheet with its four corners and sides flush/aligned with the cutting mat's grid lines. Hold the paper firmly in place to maintain alignment (or use low-tack tape on the back corners to hold it steady).

2 **Trace the line.** Using the mat's grid, measure 4" (100mm) from the paper's left vertical edge, then line up your metal straightedge along that 4" (100mm) mark. Make sure the ruler's edge is parallel to, and a tiny fraction to the left of, the 4" (100mm) mat guideline. Trace the guideline with a pencil.

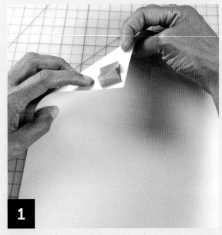

1

Align the paper.

tip: CUTTING ON THE LINE

Place your ruler ever so slightly to the left (if you are right-handed) or right (if you are left-handed) of your desired measurement grid line so that your knife blade rests exactly on the number of inches or centimeters that you need.

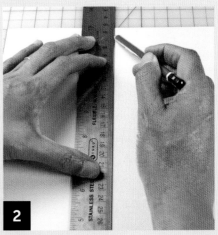

2

Trace the line.

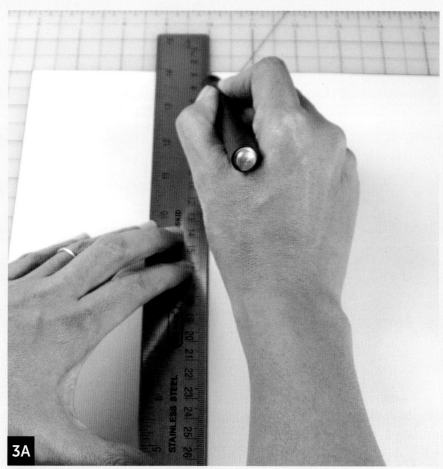

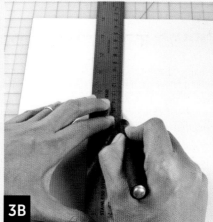

3B

3C

3A

Cut along the line.

3 **Cut the line.** Be sure the paper is lined up along all four corners, then spread your non-cutting hand's thumb and index finger widely and firmly on the ruler to hold it steady. Position the blade tip touching and parallel to—but not angled into—the ruler. Guide the blade along the ruler's edge and cut, pushing down and through. Don't remove your non-cutting hand from the ruler until the paper is completely cut free. If the blade scrapes against or sticks in the ruler, realign the blade to a parallel orientation and cut again.

4 **Cut the smaller rectangles.** You should now have two rectangles measuring 4" x 12" (100 x 305mm) each. Realign just one of the rectangles in landscape orientation on the mat. Measure 6" (150mm) across the 12" (305mm) length. Then, hold down the ruler firmly as you did above, draw the pencil guideline, and cut. You should be left with two identical 4" x 6" (100 x 150mm) rectangles. Place them atop each other to see if all 4 edges are lined up.

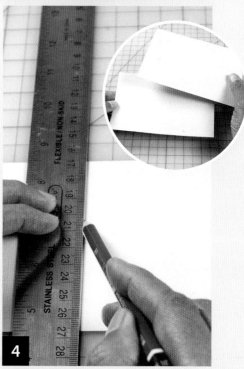

4

Trim 2 smaller rectangles.

Technique 7:
Make a master stencil

Each of this book's projects has patterns from which you'll create master stencils. Since the designs are multi-layered, each stencil corresponds to a paper layer's cutouts (except for the base layer, which is solid). Stencils allow you to craft each project more than once easily. Consider the master stencils as warm-up cutting. If your cuts are imperfect on the stencil, you can refine them as you cut the actual piece.

Practice This: Make a Master Stencil

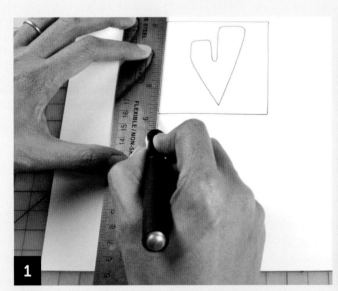

Copy and trim the stencil. Photocopy the heart in the illustration at 100%; trim it out along its 3" x 3" (75 x 75mm) border.

Shade the back. Using the side of a 2B pencil, shade the back of the illustration such that the shading corresponds to the heart outline.

tip: MASTER STENCILS

Create stencils using cardstock that is a different color than that of the actual project. For example, if the project calls for red cardstock, use light tan paper for your stencil. (Light tones such as beige or light blue will make pencil marks visible and easier to cut.) Mark each stencil "Master Stencil 1, 2, 3" etc. to indicate which stencil goes with which layer.

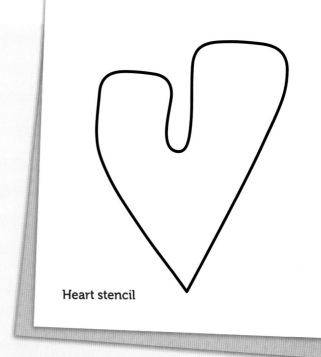

Heart stencil

3

Trace the outline onto cardstock. Flip the paper over, illustration side up, and align it atop a piece of 3" x 3" (75 x 75mm) cardstock. Hold the illustration firmly in place and trace over the heart with a sharp pencil to transfer the shading onto cardstock.

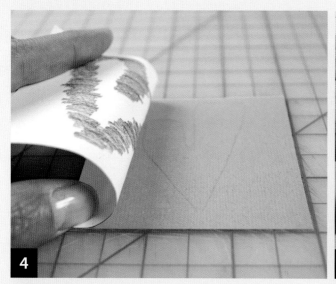

4

Check your progress. Again holding the illustration in place, lift the copy paper halfway to be sure you have transferred the entire design.

5

Cut out the stencil. Use your knife to trim out the design. Mark it "Master Stencil 1." You can now use it to create the heart shape over and over.

tip: TRANSFER PAPER

To bypass the shading process, purchase transfer paper—tracing paper coated on one side with pencil lead. Place transfer paper on top of the cardstock you'll be cutting into, then position the design atop the transfer paper and trace over the shapes. As you trace, the pencil lead will transfer the images onto the cardstock.

Technique 8:
Glue and burnish paper layers

Here are some tricks to applying glue to ensure best craftsmanship. The key is to apply as little glue as possible in thin, almost-dotted lines. Though you can try any paper-safe liquid adhesive, I highly recommend Tombow Mono Multi Liquid Glue because it adheres beautifully and has a tiny applicator tip, which allows for relatively easy repositioning. If you apply too much glue, the excess will ooze out from the sides or buckle the paper. Instead, lightly squeeze and drag the glue in a scribbling motion. Cover the entire back surface of each paper layer so that fragile or small pieces don't flap up and tear as you erase pencil marks in the final stage of your design.

Practice This: Adhere One Layer to Another

1

Create the top layer. Using the heart motif stencil you created on page 28, create a simple heart pattern on a 6" x 6" (150 x 150mm) sheet of red cardstock. Nest the hearts upside down and right side up as shown in the photo.

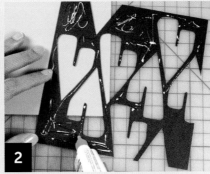

2

Cut the top layer and then the second layer. Cut out the heart shapes. Next, cut a blue 6" x 6" (150mm x 150mm) square. On the back of the red layer, apply glue in a light, scribbling motion, making sure to reach the thin spaces between each heart motif.

3

Adhere the two layers. Flip the red cardstock over, align it above the blue, then lay the two layers together.

tip: DELICATE GLUE APPLICATION

The glue applicator tip is very small, but for ultra-thin paper areas, you can squeeze glue onto scrap cardstock, dip a toothpick into it, and apply.

4

Burnish the two layers. Burnish by lightly but firmly rubbing a printing baren across the surface of the layered piece as though you were ironing fabric.

Technique 9:
Cut through multiple layers

Sometimes a project requires you to cut through more than one layer of paper or to trim down a multilayer design to fit atop a binder, box top, or note card. Though it may be daunting, the key is to start with a fresh blade and cut in multiple passes rather than attempting to shear in a single stroke. Be sure to keep the metal ruler firmly in place until the trimmed portion completely separates from the "parent" piece.

Practice This: Trim a Two-Ply Square

Try trimming ½" (15mm) from the 6" x 6" (150 x 150mm) red and blue heart piece you created in the previous practice. First, align the square on your cutting mat. Lay a metal ruler ½" (15mm) from the right edge of the square, a fraction to the left or right of the grid line (opposite of your dominant hand). Spread the thumb and forefingers of your non-cutting hand along the ruler, press it down firmly, and remember not to remove your hand until the paper is cut completely free. Now, cut along the grid line with reasonably firm pressure, once only. Reposition the blade back at the top of the grid line; you should be able to feel where your first pass indented the paper. Draw the knife down again, and perhaps a third time, until the trimmed piece separates on its own.

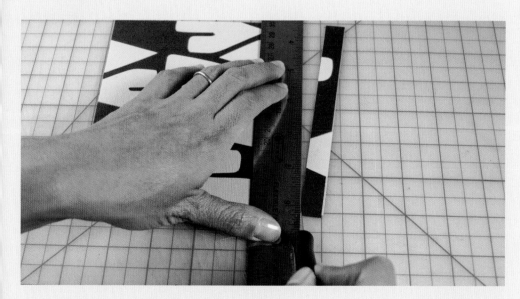

Cut through multi-layers in more than one pass. Make multiple passes with the knife using normal pressure until the trimmed piece separates on its own.

Technique 10:
Clean up your artwork

Your finished crafts will look their neatest if you erase stencil lines and remove dried glue. Luckily, adhesive pick-up squares are designed to remove both. Remember two key things when erasing: instead of rubbing back and forth, *pull in one direction only;* and wait until glue dries *before* erasing it. Think of this as a "dab-and-pull" motion, akin to blotting. This is especially important on areas with delicate cuts, where it's easy to lift up and tear the top paper layers.

Practice This: Proper Erasing

1 Erase pencil marks. Using the two-layer heart design you created and trimmed earlier, locate all remaining pencil marks. Place the top of your eraser on one of the marks and pull across the paper once. Replace it at the starting point and pull in the same direction. Repeat, gently, until the marks are gone. Continue in this way until all pencil marks are erased.

2 Remove glue spots. If there aren't any dried glue spots, create one by dabbing the slightest dot of glue anywhere on the heart design. Smear it slightly with your finger and wait for a full 3 minutes until the glue dries clear. Dab and pull at the glue spot. Don't worry if the glue turns dark first—this is simply leftover pencil lead. Keep dabbing and pulling until the eraser balls up the glue. Lift it away.

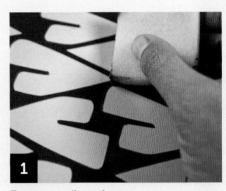

Erase pencil marks.

Remove dried glue spots.

tip: ERASING

"Brace, then erase." You're likely to have lots of little stray pencil marks from stenciling. Wait to erase until you've glued one layer onto another so that the fine little paper "bridges" and "alleys" will be braced firmly on to the paper they're adhered to. Use the corner of your adhesive pick-up square in a combination blotting/rubbing motion.

Technique 11:
Score and fold

To score paper, create a slight indentation or depression to help it bend. I discovered that using the dull side of the craft blade with about 30% of normal cutting pressure creates score lines that are useful for folded notecards, folders, and place cards. Practice here to get a feel for how much pressure you'll need to create the right indentation. Too little and the card won't fold crisply. Too much and the score line will crack through.

Practice This: Score and Fold

1 **Score the paper.** Align a 4" x 5" (100 x 130mm) piece of scrap cardstock in landscape orientation on the cutting mat. Measure and lightly pencil a line halfway or 2½" (65mm) across the 5" (130mm) edge. Keeping the metal ruler at that 2½" (65mm) pencil mark, lightly guide the unsharpened side of your craft blade along the score line.

2 **Fold the paper.** Fold the paper over along the score line and use a fingertip or baren to crease the fold.

1B

1A

Score the paper.

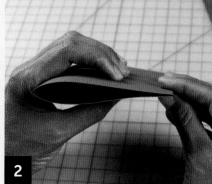
2

Fold the paper.

Technique 12:
Make square corners round

Rounded corners lend paper crafts a finished, chic look. Many of the book's projects suggest that you use a ¼" (6mm)-radius corner rounder to accomplish this.

Practice This: Punch a Corner

Insert any rectangular or square piece of cardstock into the corner punch (see p. 16 for recommended model) until you feel the paper hit the punch's back edge. Depress the button; there should be a sharp click/thunk. Remove the paper and check your corner. If the cut is at all jagged, simply reinsert the paper, push until it's as far back into the punch as possible, and depress the button again.

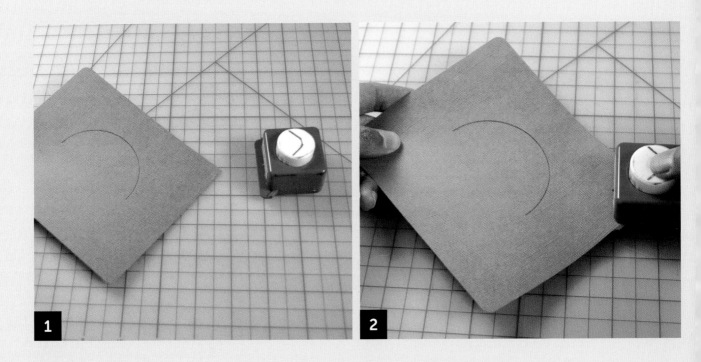

Technique 13:
Modify a pattern template

One reason I love making patterns is the endless creativity that comes from rearranging a single motif in multiple configurations. I provide you with stencil patterns and exact dimensions, but I invite you to resize or compose a motif to lend a pattern a different feeling. For starters you can play with proportion by copying the pattern at a slightly larger or smaller percentage than 100% to place atop various objects. See below for other ways to play with patterns.

Try This: Trim Down the Design and Recycle the Leftovers

Say you want to upcycle an old notebook, binder, or blank note card that's smaller than the pattern I've provided. Simply complete the project as I instruct, then apply Technique 9 (p. 31) to trim the project to the exact size you need. Depending on the dimensions of the leftover trim, you can create a bonus item or two. I've created gift tags, note card borders, and even bookmarks from so-called scraps.

Try This: Change the Pattern Layout

There are so many ways to repeat a motif to turn it into a pattern. Rather than using a "negative space" stencil composed inside a border, try using a single "positive space" motif to play around with alternate arrangements. Notice how I took a single duckbill motif and arranged it in stacked and circular patterns. Browse through pattern design books for ideas or create your own. One of my favorites is *Textile Designs: Two Hundred Years of European and American Patterns Organized by Motif, Style, Color, Layout and Period* (Abrams, 2002).

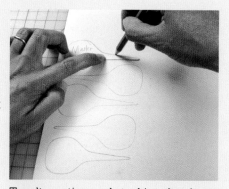

Try alternating and stacking the shapes.

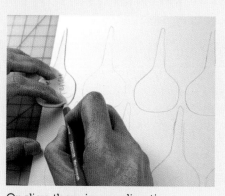

Or align them in one direction.

CONGRATULATIONS!

You've completed the tutorials. You are now ready to measure, stencil, cut, layer, and glue your way to some seriously beautiful paper crafts.

chapter 1

Tabletop Stationery

* * * * * * * * * * * * * * * * *

As a former chef and avid home cook, I love combining the

culinary and paper arts. The projects in this chapter feature layered

paper pieces you can use as the ultimate food accessories. Long

after the last crumb is gone, the designs are tactile keepsakes of

your most joyful occasions.

Modern Blooms Cake Wrap, page 56
PHOTO BY LISA FRANCHOT.

PHOTO BY LISA FRANCHOT

Dessert Stencils

When I look at a brownie, I see a gorgeous chocolate canvas waiting to be decorated. You'll be surprised at how easy it is to create homemade food stencils simply by covering cardstock with clear adhesive paper, trimming out the motifs, and dusting powdered sugar over the stencils onto brownies. The resulting crisp white hearts and flowers will dazzle you and your guests. Keep stencils handy to transform brownies into magical treats for birthdays and holidays.

Culinary Stencils: Best-dressed Brownies. I was enchanted to learn about food stencils that required just powdered sugar and a sieve, so I created my own using four motifs. With just a little shake, you can turn brownies into miniature edible works of art.

NOTE ABOUT BROWNIE DIMENSIONS

Most brownie recipes call for a 9" x 13" (230 x 330mm) baking pan, which reflects the pan's *top* dimensions. As you will decorate the *bottom* of the brownies, note that the pan bottom measures closer to 8" x 12" (205 x 305mm).

CARDSTOCK CUTTING LIST

Any color cardstock (master stencils): 12" x 12" (305 x 305mm) square

TOOLS AND MATERIALS

- 1 batch brownies, baked and cooled completely
- Confectioner's sugar
- Fine wire mesh sieve
- Clear/transparent adhesive paper, such as Con-tact Paper
- Metal ruler
- Craft knife, such as X-ACTO knife
- Blades for craft knife, such as X-ACTO #11 blades
- 2B pencil
- Self-healing cutting mat

CREATING A FOIL SLING

Sugar designs show up best on the bottom of the brownies, so it's essential to create a foil sling to lift brownies out of the pan neatly. Before pouring brownie batter into a 13" x 9" (330 x 230mm) pan, firmly press an 18" (470mm)-long piece of foil lengthwise across the pan, allowing the excess foil to come up the sides. Next, press and overlap two 14" (355mm)-long foil pieces perpendicular to the 18" (470mm)-foil piece, allowing the extra foil to come up the sides. Spray with non-stick baking spray. Bake brownies and allow them to cool in the pan for at least an hour. Use the sling to lift the entire brownie cake out of the pan and let it cool again for at least half an hour before flipping and cutting.

Prepare the brownies and trim all paper elements to size. Bake your favorite recipe for chocolate brownies in a foil sling (see pg. 39) and remove them from the pan when completely cool. While they are cooling, prepare the stencils. Cut a 5" x 5" (130 x 130mm) piece of cardstock. Draw a line down the middle of each side, forming 4 squares measuring 2½" x 2½" (65 x 65mm) each. Cut a 10" x 7" (255 x 180mm) rectangle of contact paper and set aside.

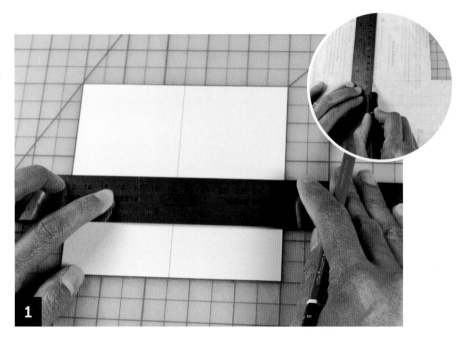

1

2

Create the stencil. Photocopy and transfer the 4 decorative motifs (rose, hearts, orchid, spiral flower) to the 5" x 5" (130 x 130mm) square.

3

Cover the stencil with clear adhesive paper. Fold the contact paper rectangle in half along the 10" (255mm) edge. Sharply crease the fold. Peel the contact paper from its backing up to the fold. Position one of the stencil's edges flush against the fold, leaving about a 1" (25mm) contact paper border around the stencil's other 3 edges. Lay the stencil on the contact adhesive. Peel back the remaining half of the contact paper and cover the other side of the cardstock. Smooth out any bubbles. Trim off contact paper just to the edge of the cardstock.

Cut out the motifs. Use a fresh blade to cut through the two-ply layer of cardstock and contact paper. When releasing each shape, be sure to cut through, rather than pull on, the double layer of contact paper and cardstock to create clear, crisp stencil edges.

Trim to separate the four individual stencils. Cut the stencil grid along the straight lines so that it renders 4 separate 2½" x 2½" (65mm) stencil squares. Flip the entire cooled brownie cake onto a cutting board such that the cake bottom is facing up. Peel away the foil sling and use a chef's knife to lightly mark the cake every 2½" (65mm) across and 2½" (65mm) down. Cut as many brownies as possible (you should have about 12–14).

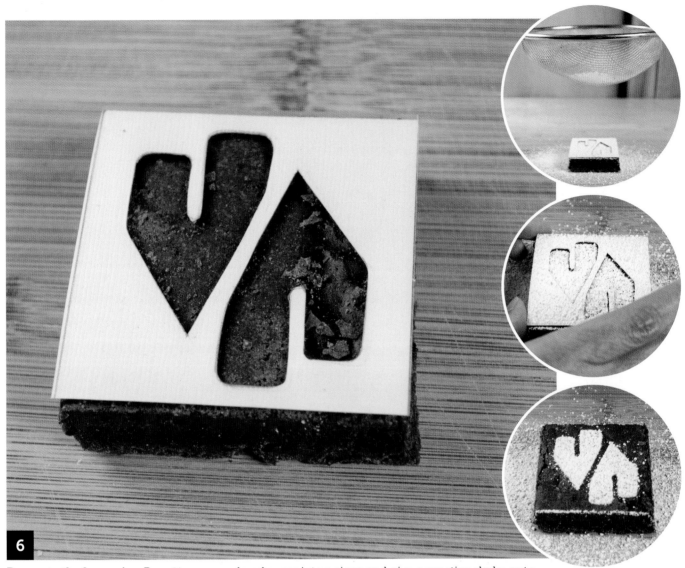

6

Decorate the brownies. Pour ¼ cup powdered sugar into a sieve and give a practice shake onto a plate. Place a single brownie onto the plate with one of the stencils resting atop it. Lightly dust the sugar so that it fills the shape of the motif. With two fingertips, carefully lift the stencil off the brownie. Clean the sugar off both stencil and plate each time you decorate.

tip: SUGAR APPLICATION

Shake the sugar lightly just so it fills in the stencil cutouts. If you shake too much, the sugar will pile up and slide downward after your remove the stencil, creating blurry rather than crisp silhouettes. Also, use a very steady hand when lifting off the stencil to avoid excess sugar falling on your brownie and muddying the motif.

Dessert Stencil patterns: Orchid, Hearts, Spiral Flower, Rose

You Can Also Try:

Creating a Multi-Window Stencil

For larger quantities of brownies, create a grid of stencils to speed the decorating process. Draw a grid of 12 stencil squares (4 across x 3 down). Repeat the motifs of your choice to fill all 12 squares. Cut enough contact paper to cover the cardstock plus a 1" (25mm) border that extends beyond the stencil. Cut the motifs out of the grid, but leave the rectangle whole rather than dividing it into individual stencils. Place the stencil over the entire un-cut brownie cake, shake the sugar over the entire sheet, and cut the brownie squares.

Stenciling Numbers or Letters

For birthdays or other celebrations, consider creating stencils of letters or numbers that spell the celebrant's name or age. Arrange the squares into the message and the flower and heart motifs around it.

YIELD: 24 toppers (12 girls, 12 boys), 2½" x 2" (65 x 50mm) each

Cupcake Toppers

I love to cook almost as much as I love to cut paper, and for family birthdays, I tend to bake cupcakes. For kids' parties, try these friendly paper-cut cupcake toppers featuring Little Bow Peep and her counterpart, Cowlick Boy. I kept the design to two layers with simple cuts because you'll be cutting in quantity. Increase or decrease amounts as needed, and feel free to adapt my suggested color ways to suit your party theme. The toppers' modern, chic style even appeals to adults.

CARDSTOCK CUTTING LIST

Any color cardstock (master stencils): (3) 2½" x 2" (65 x 50mm) rectangles

Little Bow Peep

- Apple green cardstock (bottom layer): 6" x 12" (150 x 305mm) rectangle
- Butter yellow cardstock (top layer): 6" x 12" (150 x 305mm) rectangle
- Lavender cardstock (bows): 6" x 6" (150 x 150mm) square

Cowlick Boy

- Apple green cardstock (top layer): 6" x 12" (150 x 305mm) rectangle
- Royal blue cardstock (bottom layer): 6" x 12" (150 x 305mm) rectangle

TOOLS AND MATERIALS

- (24) wooden toothpicks
- (24) 3-D glue dots (or clear tape)
- ¼" (6mm)-radius corner punch rounder
- Metal ruler
- Craft knife, such as X-ACTO knife

- Blades for craft knife, such as X-ACTO #11 blades
- 2B pencil
- Adhesive pick-up square
- Liquid adhesive for paper
- Self-healing cutting mat

Cupcake Toppers: Best Cupcake Companions. My daughter's first self-portraits featured herself with a giant hair bow, which I translated into this Little Bow Peep motif. I designed her companion, Cowlick Boy (whose hair quirk I sometimes share!).

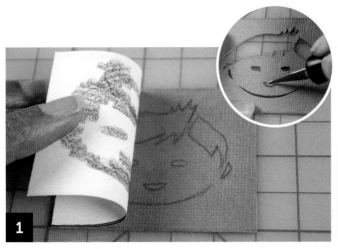

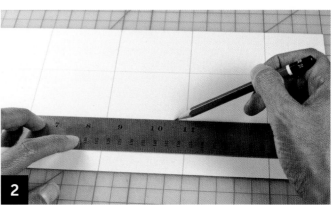

1

Transfer and cut each master stencil. Trim the cardstock to the specifications shown on the cutting list. Photocopy and transfer the little girl, boy, and bow designs to the master stencil rectangles. Cut out the shapes.

2

Draw grids on the cardstock. With the yellow 12" x 6" (305 x 150mm) sheet in landscape orientation, pencil 4 grid lines every 2½" (65mm) across and 2 grid lines every 2" (50mm) down. You should have a grid consisting of 12 rectangles that measure 2½" x 2" (65 x 50mm) each. Trim off the very last 2" (50mm)-wide column. Draw an identical grid on one of the green 12" x 6" (305 x 150mm) layers.

3

Cut the yellow Bow Peep layer and green Cowlick Boy layer. Position the Bow Peep master stencil inside the top left rectangle on the yellow cardstock. Draw in the girl pattern 12 times. Use the same process to stencil in the Cowlick Boy on the green cardstock. Cut out the stenciled shapes.

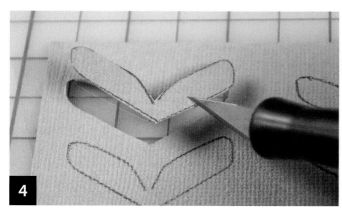

4

Cut the bows. On the lavender cardstock, stencil in 12 bows and cut them out.

5

Adhere the two layers for both Bow Peep and Cowlick Boy. For Bow Peep: Apply glue to the back of the yellow sheet, align it with the remaining green layer, adhere the two, and burnish. For Cowlick Boy: Repeat with the green apple and royal blue sheets.

6

Trim out the toppers. Follow guidelines for trimming multiple layers (pg. 31) to align and trim the cardstock along the grid lines.

tip: KEEP STENCILING ACCURATE

Maintain original stencil width. Re-sharpen your pencil if it gets dull so that the stenciled-in tiny eye and mouth shapes don't get too thick.

7

Round all corners (optional). Punch round corners to complement the cupcakes' roundness.

8

Glue on bows. Apply glue to each purple bow and position each atop the little girl's hair. Burnish.

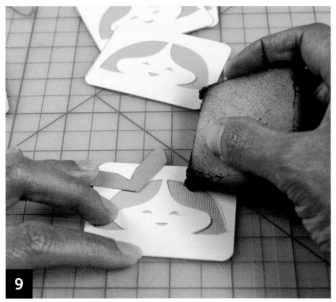

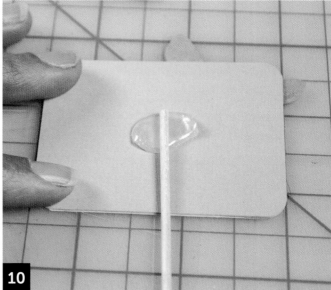

9

Clean up the artwork. Use the adhesive pickup square to remove pencil marks and glue.

10

Attach toothpicks. Place a 3D glue dot on the back center of each rectangle. Wedge a toothpick firmly in the glue dot and insert the finished toppers into cupcakes.

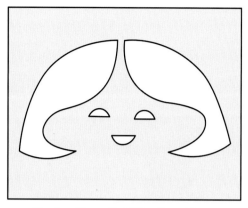

Master Stencil: Little Bow Peep

Master Stencil: Cowlick Boy

Master Stencil: Bows

You Can Also Try:

Recycling the Hair Shapes
In Step 3, save yourself cutting time by reusing the hair shapes set aside after the first time you did this project. Cut out the eyes, mouth, and ears, and then proceed with the rest of the steps.

Making Baby Shower Place Cards
Cut and score place card tents as described on page 33, then stencil in the Little Bow Peep or Cowlick Boy on the card, leaving space for names. Cut out each boy and girl motif, and then adhere 2½" x 4" (65 x 100mm) rectangles beneath the place card flap. Add a bow to Little Bow Peep.

Adding a Number
Create your own master stencil for the numeral representing your child's age. Cut out this numeral 24 times and glue it to each topper.

Recycle hair shapes.

Decorating a Child's or Baby Shower Gift
Use a glue dot to attach the topper in the center of a wrapped gift where you would normally place a bow.

PHOTO BY LISA FRANCHOT

'A Cut Above' Place Cards

Even at low-key dinner parties with casual seating, guests are charmed at seeing their names on place cards. I designed these table tents with delicate hand-cut motifs to set off a name with simple, elegant flair. For this project, you'll cut assorted motifs and suspend them slightly off the cards' edges to enhance their see-through beauty. You could write buffet dish names or table numbers on them, too. If your guests are like mine, they may take them home as lovely souvenirs.

Place Cards: Places, Please. This eclectic assortment of motifs includes a rose, snowflake, bellflower, and steaming soup bowl floating atop buttery yellow table tents in earthy, yummy tones to complement any buffet.

CARDSTOCK CUTTING LIST

- Any color cardstock (master stencils): (8) 3½" x 3½" (90 x 90mm) squares
- Crimson red cardstock (roses): (2) 3½" x 3½" (90 x 90mm) squares
- Deep orange cardstock (snowflakes): (2) 3½" x 3½" (90 x 90mm) squares
- Goldenrod yellow cardstock (bellflowers): (2) 3½" x 3½" (90 x 90mm) squares
- Espresso brown cardstock (steaming soup bowls): (2) 3½" x 3½" (90 x 90mm) squares
- Butter yellow cardstock (place card bases): (8) 4" x 5" (100 x 130mm) rectangles

PHOTO BY LISA FRANCHOT

Variety Show: Try using all 4 designs in a single place setting just for fun. From front to back: Steaming bowl, bellflower, botanical snowflake, rose.

TOOLS AND MATERIALS

- ¼" (6mm) radius corner punch rounder
- Metal ruler
- Craft knife, such as X-ACTO knife
- Blades for craft knife, such as X-ACTO #11 blades
- 2B pencil
- Adhesive pick-up square
- Liquid adhesive for paper

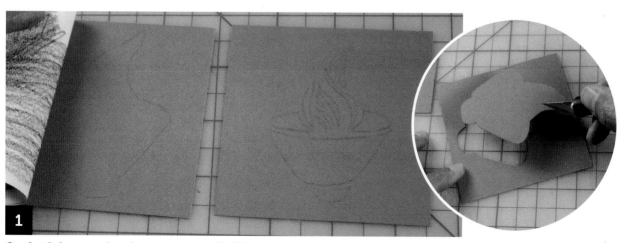

Cut both layers of each master stencil. Trim the cardstock to the specifications shown on the cutting list. Photocopy and transfer each design to light-colored cardstock. To avoid tearing, cut from the center toward the outer shapes. Mark the squares "Master Stencil, Rose 1," "Master Stencil, Rose 2," "Master Stencil, Snowflake 1," "Master Stencil, Snowflake 2," etc.

Cut the motifs. Use each pair of master stencils to cut two of each motif. Match the stencil to the color given in the cutting list. Begin by tracing "Master Stencil, Steaming Bowl 1" on brown cardstock. Align "Master Stencil, Steaming Bowl 2" atop your first set of lines. Trace the silhouette. Cut out all lines, working from the center toward the outer silhouette. Pop out the entire shape. Repeat with each motif.

note:

Each motif requires two master stencils: one for interior shapes and the second for the exterior silhouette. This two-step stencil maintains a border for your hand to hold the stencil steady while making intricate, delicate cuts.

Score and fold place cards. Draw score lines 2½" (65mm) or halfway across the 5" (130mm) edge of the yellow rectangles. Score and fold them such that each forms a table tent with 2 flaps measuring 2½" x 4" (65 x 100mm) each. Use a fingernail or baren to crease the fold.

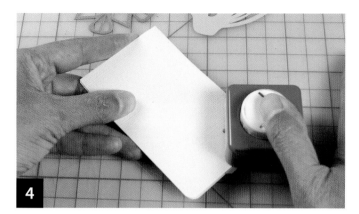

4

Round the place card corners (optional). With place cards still folded in half, use a corner punch to round all 4 corners of each card.

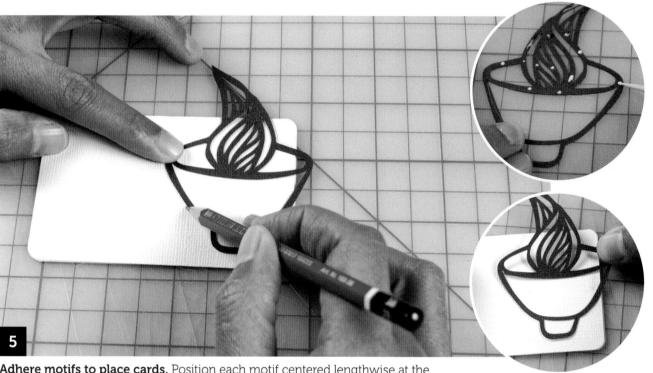

5

Adhere motifs to place cards. Position each motif centered lengthwise at the right of each card. Lightly trace around the motif to mark its position. Apply glue in light dotted lines to the back of each motif—but only to the portion that will rest atop the card. Use a toothpick dipped in glue if necessary. Flip the motif right side up and re-position it within the markings. Adhere and burnish.

6

Clean up the artwork. Use the adhesive pick-up square to remove pencil marks and dried glue.

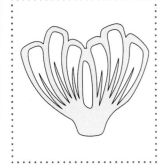

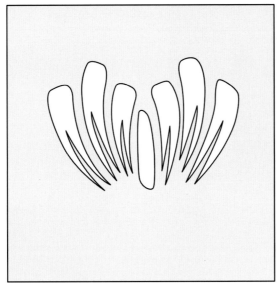

Master Stencil 1: Bellflower
Copy at 130%

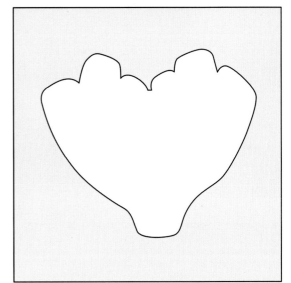

Master Stencil 2: Bellflower
Copy at 130%

Master Stencil 1: Rose
Copy at 130%

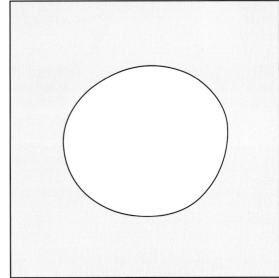

Master Stencil 2: Rose
Copy at 130%

tip: MASTER STENCILS

Remember to use the Master Stencil 1 first for each project so you have as much border to hold onto as possible while cutting out the delicate interior cuts.

Master Stencil 1: Snowflake
Copy at 130%

Master Stencil 2: Snowflake
Copy at 130%

Master Stencil 1: Steaming Bowl
Copy at 130%

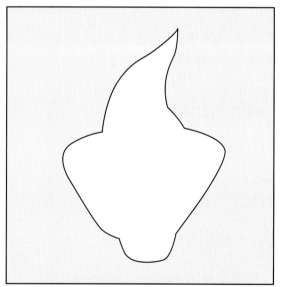

Master Stencil 2: Steaming Bowl
Copy at 130%

You Can Also Try:

Turning Motifs into Embellishments
The hand-cut motifs on their own can serve as embellishments. Try using a glue dot to attach one to a gift ribbon in place of a bow, or to scrapbook pages, envelopes, note cards, etc.

Modifying Color Combinations
If you use a single motif, such as a rose, consider cutting it in a variety of colors. Alternately, cut all four motifs from a single color.

Modern Blooms Cake Wrap

Here's another way to bring the beauty of paper cuts to your tabletop: a cake wrap that adds graphic punch to birthday and wedding cakes, or to a tower of dessert bars. I designed this wrap for a 13" (330mm)-diameter display stand, but you can easily adapt it for smaller or larger sizes, or even a square stand. The rose motifs may look complex, but they are really just crescent shapes nested in a circle. Cut delicate green leaves and collage them on top to form a richly layered, tactile keepsake that lasts long after the party is over.

CARDSTOCK CUTTING LIST

Any color cardstock (Master Stencil 1): 2½" x 12" (65 x 305mm) rectangle
Any color cardstock (Master Stencil 2): 2" x 2" (50 x 50mm) square

- Butter yellow cardstock (top layer):
  (4) 2½" x 12" (65 x 305mm) rectangles
- Goldenrod yellow cardstock (bottom layer):
  (4) 2½" x 12" (65 x 305mm) rectangles

- Grass green cardstock (leaves):
  6" x 6" (150 x 150mm) square

TOOLS AND MATERIALS

- 13" (330mm)-diameter round cake stand
- 3-D glue dots
- Tape measure
- ¾" (20mm) artist's tape
- Metal ruler
- Craft knife, such as X-ACTO knife

- Blades for craft knife, such as X-ACTO #11 blades
- 2B pencil
- Adhesive pick-up square
- Liquid adhesive for paper

Cake Wrap: Nested Crescents. The delicious yellow roses of Modern Blooms grace this cake wrap and reveal my penchant for nested shapes, in this case, crescents. Cut and hang simple green leaves off the edges for a dimensional effect. The piece dresses up dessert for any occasion.

NOTE ON CAKE STAND DIMENSIONS:

If you're using a 13" (330mm) diameter cake stand, the finished wrap should measure 2½" (65mm) high and 42" (1m) long. Follow the directions below to create a 2½" (65mm) x 48" (1.2m) wrap (extra just in case) and trim off the excess 6" (150mm) to fit.

If your cake stand has a diameter smaller or larger than 13" (330mm), measure your cake stand circumference exactly by placing glue dots every 2"–3" (50–75mm) around the stand and wrap a tape measure around it, using the glue dots to hold it in place. Note its length and make necessary adjustments. I suggest adding 1" (25mm) to the cake wrap length just in case.

If you are using a square stand, measure one of the square's edges and cut Master Stencil 1 (and each yellow strip) to that length. Most scrapbook cardstock comes no longer than 12" (305mm), so if the edge is longer than that, you will need to use oversized artist's paper (See Resources, p. 142).

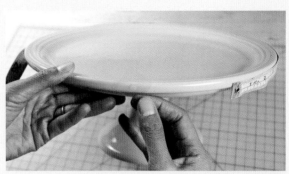

Prepare the rose stencil. Trim the cardstock to the specifications shown on the cutting list. Photocopy the rose design at 125% and transfer the design to a 2½" x 12" (65 x 305mm) strip. Cut out the shapes. Label it "Master Stencil 1."

1

Cut the pale/butter yellow layer. Align Master Stencil 1 on one of the butter yellow 2½" x 12" (65 x 305mm) rectangles. Transfer the design and cut out each rose. Repeat this process with the remaining three butter yellow rectangles.

2

3 Adhere the pale and goldenrod/deep yellow layers. Apply glue to a pale yellow rectangle. Align it with a goldenrod rectangle, adhere, and burnish. Repeat this process with the remaining three pale yellow and three deep yellow rectangles.

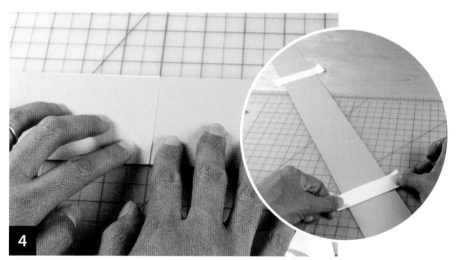

4 Hinge all four paper strips into a single wrap. Cut three 3" (75mm) strips of artist's tape and set aside. Place the yellow rectangles in the same orientation—flush, but not overlapping. Flip the rectangles over such that their back sides face up and the edges are lined up. Hinge all three seams, letting tape extend ½" (15mm) over the top and bottom edges of the paper.

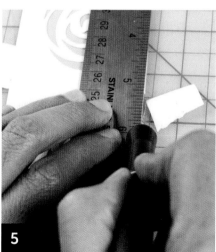

5 Trim off excess tape. Flip the now 48" (1.2m)-long strip over, lay your metal ruler just to the paper edges, and carefully trim off excess tape.

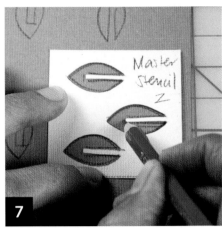

Create the Leaf Master Stencil. Photocopy and transfer the 3 leaf shapes onto the 2" x 2" (50 x 50mm) square cardstock of any color. Cut out the leaves and mark this "Master Stencil 2."

Cut out the leaves. Place Master Stencil 2 onto the 6" x 6" (150 x 150mm) green square and draw the leaf trio six times for a total of eighteen leaves. Cut them out.

Adhere the leaves. Dot the backside of each leaf with glue, then use your blade tip to place them artfully around the rose motifs. Let some hang off the edges for a dimensional effect. After confirming your cake stand's circumference, add 1" (25mm) to that measurement and trim your wrap to that length. This will allow you to overlap the wrap slightly.

Attach the cake wrap to the stand. Attach glue dots along the stand's rim every 2–3" (50–75mm). Beginning with the cake wrap's left edge, press the wrap into the glue dots, flattening as you go. Overlap the wrap's right end slightly over the left end.

You Can Also Try:

Cutting Scalloped Edges

In Step 2, lightly pencil connected half-circles under each rose motif, creating a scalloped border. Cut along the sketch lines. In Step 3, after you have adhered the light and darker yellow layers, pencil half-circles onto the darker yellow layer that rest just below the scalloped shapes of the lighter yellow layer. Trim the paper along those scalloped edges and proceed with Step 4.

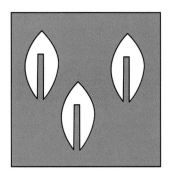

Master Stencil 2: Leaves
Copy at 125%

Master Stencil 1: Roses

Note: Copying this pattern requires the use of legal-size paper (it's a bit over the 11½" [290mm] length of a normal piece of paper).

Copy at 125%

chapter 2

Gifts and Holidays

* * * * * * * * * * * * * * * * *

So often it's handmade gifts and holiday decorations that become

our most treasured household items because we recognize the

time and love that went into their creation. As you cut the master

stencils for these paper gems, know that you can use them again

and again for holidays, birthdays, graduations, weddings, and all

of life's milestones.

Festive Holiday Ornament Trio, page 78

Teardrop Vine Journals

Beautiful journals have inspired me to sit down and write, make lists, and daydream. Here's a gift for writers who want to encase their words in beauty: a pair of tactile, boldly graphic journals covered in a gently meandering vine pattern in both forest and red-blue jewel tones. Use the same pair of master stencils to craft

5" x 8" (130 x 205mm) layered pattern cover art, and then adhere both to kraft paper journals. The lucky recipient can also trim off the cover art and frame one or both. This project is a great way to refresh or upcycle any journal, notebook, or sketch pad.

CARDSTOCK CUTTING LIST

Any color cardstock (master stencils): (2) 5" x 8" (130 x 205mm) rectangles

Forest tones journal

- Espresso brown cardstock (top layer): 5" x 8" (130 x 205mm) rectangle
- Pale green cardstock (middle layer): 5" x 8" (130 x 205mm) rectangle
- Dark grass green cardstock (bottom layer): 5" x 8" (130 x 205mm) rectangle

Red-blue jewel tones journal

- Crimson red cardstock (top layer): 5" x 8" (130 x 205mm) rectangle
- Pale blue cardstock: (middle layer): 5" x 8" (130 x 205mm) rectangle
- Royal blue cardstock (bottom layer): 5" x 8" (130 x 205mm) rectangle

TOOLS AND MATERIALS

- (2) 5" x 8" (130 x 205mm) paper-covered journals, preferably recycled kraft paper (See Resources, p. 142)
- Self-healing cutting mat
- Metal ruler
- Craft knife, such as X-ACTO knife
- Blades for craft knife, such as X-ACTO #11 blades
- 2B pencil
- Adhesive pick-up square
- Liquid adhesive for paper

Decorative Journals: Design for Inspired Writing. I found on my cutting mat a teardrop-shaped scrap from a previous project and tried using it as a stencil, repeating the shape along a vine, the way ivy climbs on the side of a building. This Teardrop Vine pattern was born, and it meanders nicely across these journals, too.

Prepare the Teardrop Vine master stencil. Trim the cardstock to the specifications on the cutting list. Photocopy and transfer the teardrop vine pattern to the 5" x 8" (130 x 205mm) cardstock. Cut out the shapes and mark this "Master Stencil 1."

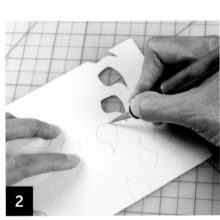

Prepare the Leaf Interior master stencil. Photocopy and transfer the leaf interior pattern to the 5" x 8" (130 x 205mm) cardstock. Cut out the shapes and mark this "Master Stencil 2."

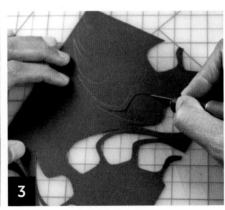

Cut the top layer. Align Master Stencil 1 atop the dark brown [or red] 5" x 8" (130 x 205mm) layer, draw in the design, and cut out the shapes.

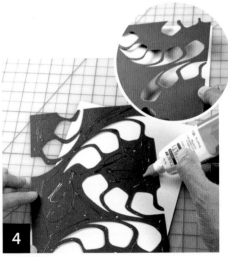

Adhere the top and middle layers. Apply glue to the back of the brown [or red] layer. Align the brown and pale green [or the red and pale blue] layers, lay them together, and burnish. Trim off overhanging edges if necessary.

5

6

Cut the middle layer. Align Master Stencil 2 atop the two-ply brown-green or red-blue sheet. Lightly draw in the design. See that the leaf shapes you drew are spaced properly inside the top layer's shapes. Erase and redraw any shapes that fell out of registration and cut them out. Smooth over the surface with the baren.

Adhere the middle and bottom layers. Apply glue to the middle layer and align it with the bottom layer. Burnish.

Adhere the artwork to the journal.
Place the finished three-ply design on the journal cover. Check to see that the edges of the artwork line up with the journal. If the design is slightly larger than the cover, carefully trim off any overhanging edges.

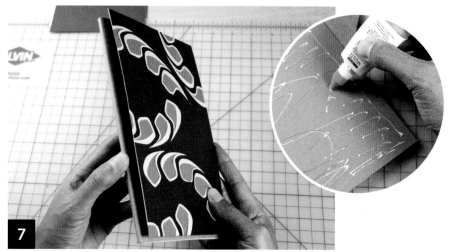

7

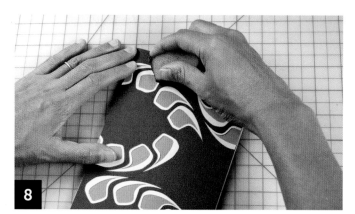

8

Clean up the artwork. Remove any pencil marks and dried glue with the adhesive pick-up square using a "dab and pull" motion.

You Can Also Try:

Turning the Cover Art into a Note Card
Skip Step 7. After Step 6, use a fresh blade to trim 1" (25mm) off the 8" (205mm) edge. You'll be left with a 5" x 7" (130 x 180mm) rectangle, the size of a standard note card. Adhere this design to a blank note card (See Resources, p. 142). Or simply make your own note card by cutting a 10" x 7" (255 x 180mm) rectangle and scoring it halfway through the 10" (255mm) edge. Fold it in half and adhere the 5" x 7" (130 x 180mm) design to the front of one of the card halves.

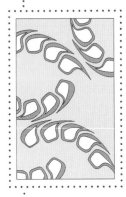

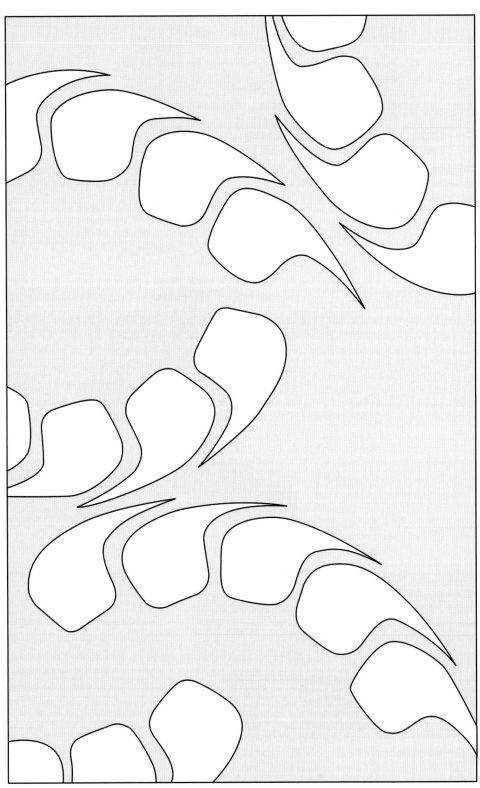

Master Stencil 1: Teardrop Vine

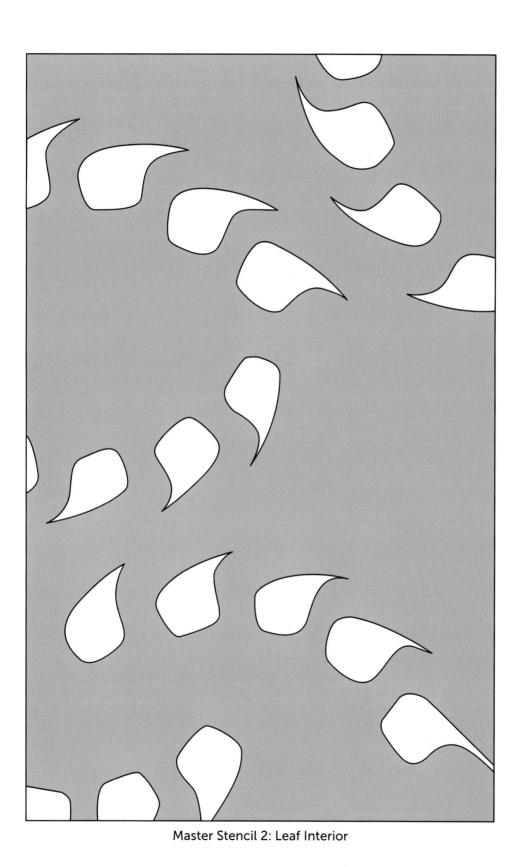

Master Stencil 2: Leaf Interior

YIELD: 3 boxes

Fruited Plane Gift Box Trio

It's easy to see why these inexpensive and sturdy papier-mâché boxes sell out regularly at my favorite craft store: with a bit of decoration they are easily transformed into charming storage. Here, I've covered the tops of this box trio (sold as a unit) with a stylized fruit/botanical design. They make good-looking organizers for paper clips, jewelry, keys, or other household odds and ends. I also keep them handy as gift boxes to avoid the last minute scramble for wrapping paper. Presented as a set, the boxes are a gift in and of themselves.

CARDSTOCK CUTTING LIST

Small box
- Any color cardstock (master stencils): (2) 4" x 4" (100 x 100mm) squares
- Crimson red cardstock (top layer): 4" x 4" (100 x 100mm) square
- Butter yellow cardstock (middle layer): 4" x 4" (100 x 100mm) square
- Aqua cardstock (bottom layer): 4" x 4" (100 x 100mm) square

Medium box
- Any color cardstock (master stencils): (2) 5" x 5" (130 x 130mm) squares
- Crimson red cardstock (top layer): 5" x 5" (130 x 130mm) square

- Butter yellow cardstock (middle layer): 5" x 5" (130 x 130mm) square
- Aqua cardstock (bottom layer): 5" x 5" (130 x 130mm) square

Large box
- Any color cardstock (master stencils): (2) 6" x 6" (150 x 150mm) squares
- Crimson red cardstock (top layer): 6" x 6" (150 x 150mm) square
- Butter yellow cardstock (middle layer): 6" x 6" (150 x 150mm) square
- Aqua cardstock (bottom layer): 6" x 6" (150 x 150mm) square

TOOLS AND MATERIALS

- (1) set of papier-mâché boxes, sizes 4" (100mm), 5" (130mm), and 6" (150mm)
- Self-healing cutting mat
- Metal ruler
- Craft knife, such as X-ACTO knife

- Blades for craft knife, such as X-ACTO #11 blades
- 2B pencil
- Adhesive pick-up square
- Liquid adhesive for paper

Decorative Storage Box Trio: Beauty in Cross-Section. The slightly mysterious motifs of this Fruited Plane design came from looking at the cross-section of a freshly cut pear. The rich red, yellow, and pale blue color combination was inspired by an image of a Chinese scholar's study.

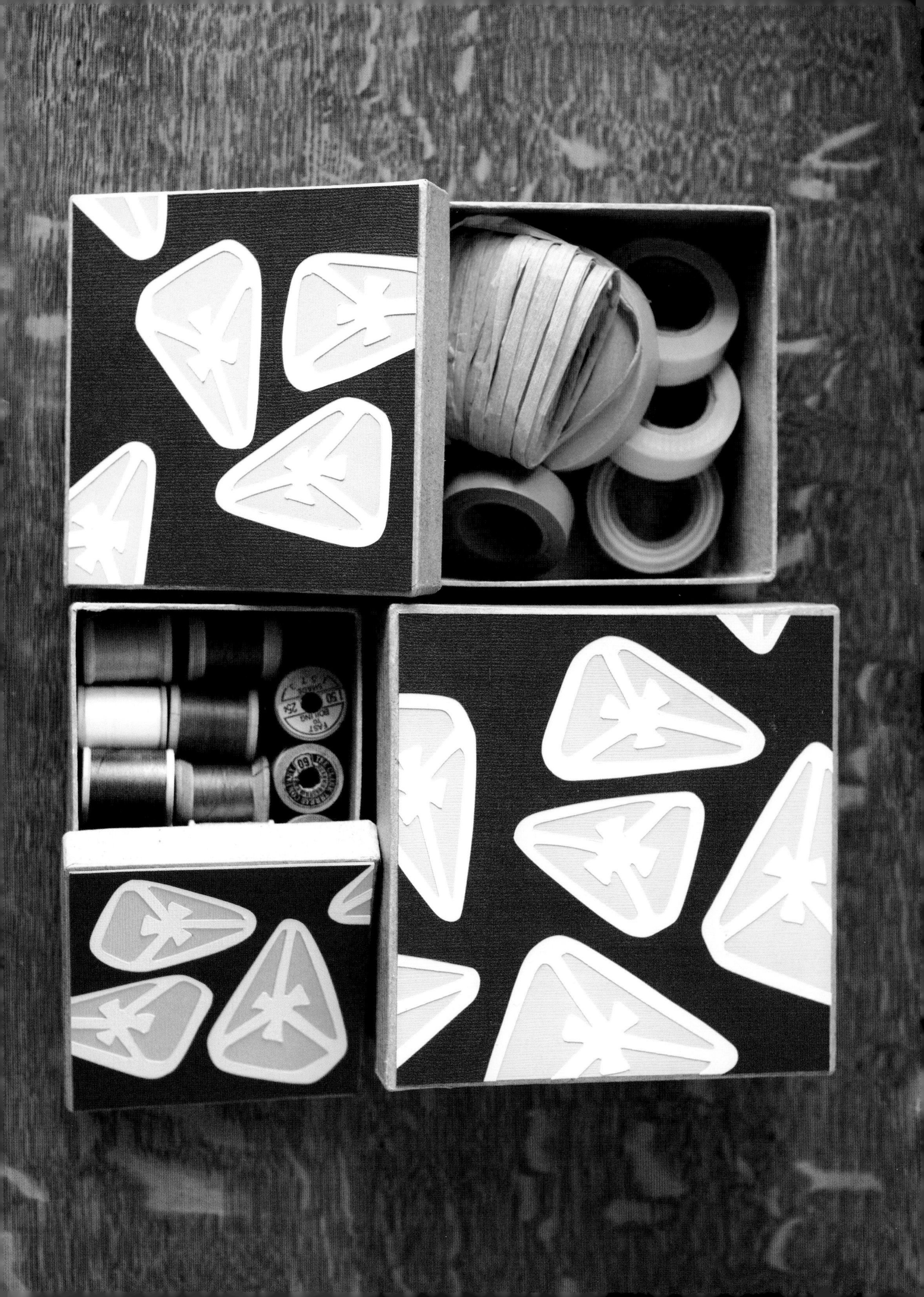
FAST TO BOILING

Prepare all three Fruit Exterior master stencils. Trim the cardstock to the specifications on the cutting list. Photocopy and transfer the small, medium, and large versions of the Fruit Exterior design to the 4" x 4" (100 x 100mm), 5" x 5" (130 x 130mm) and 6" x 6" (150 x 150mm) squares. Mark them "Master Stencil 1 (Small)," "Master Stencil 1 (Medium)," and "Master Stencil 1 (Large)."

Prepare the Fruit Interior master stencils. Photocopy and transfer the small, medium, and large versions of the Fruit Interior design to the 4" x 4" (100 x 102mm), 5" x 5" (130 x 130mm), and 6" x 6" (150 x 150mm) squares. Mark them "Master Stencil 2 (Small)," "Master Stencil 2 (Medium)," and "Master Stencil 2 (Large)."

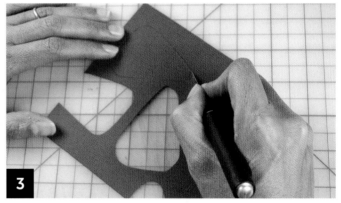

Cut the red layers. Align Master Stencil 1 (Small) atop the red 4" x 4" (100 x 100mm) square, draw in the design, and cut out the shapes. Repeat this with medium and large versions of Master Stencil 1 and the 5" x 5" (130 x 130mm) and 6" x 6" (150 x 150mm) red squares, respectively.

Adhere the red and yellow layers. Lightly apply glue to the back of all three red layers. Line up the corners of each red and corresponding yellow square, lay them together, and burnish. Carefully trim off the overhanging edges.

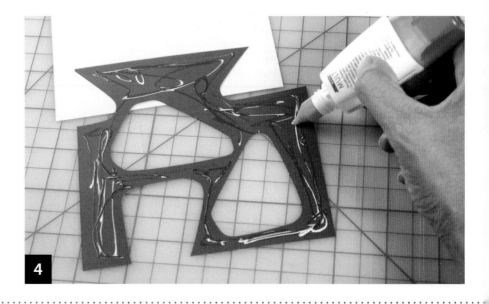

Cut the yellow layers. Align Master Stencil 2 (Small) atop the 4" x 4" (100 x 100mm) layer. Lightly stencil in the design. Erase and redraw any shapes that fell out of registration. Cut out the stenciled shapes. Repeat this process with the medium and large versions of Master Stencil 2 and the 5" x 5" (127mm x 127mm) and 6" x 6" (152mm x 152mm) yellow squares, respectively.

Adhere the yellow and aqua layers. Lightly apply glue to the back of all three yellow layers. Line up the corners of each yellow and corresponding aqua square, lay them together, and burnish. Carefully trim off any overhanging edges.

Adhere artwork to the boxes. Place each finished three-ply design on top of its corresponding box top. Be sure the edges of the artwork line up with each box cover. If any are slightly larger than the box top, trim off any overhanging edges.

tip: STENCILS ARE GUIDES

No one ever cuts out a stencil exactly along the pencil lines. For that reason, your stenciled middle layer may not line up perfectly within the first layer. Consider your stencils a guide: it's less important to follow the pencil sketch slavishly and more important to pay attention to how your cuts lie in relation to the first layer's shapes.

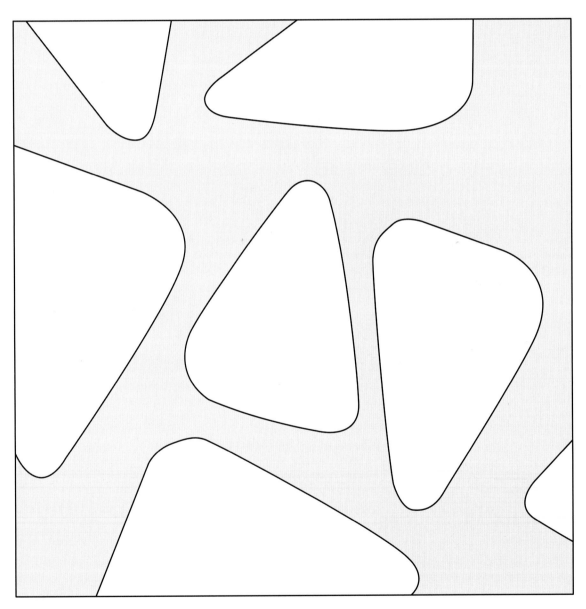

Master Stencil 1 (Large): Fruit Exterior

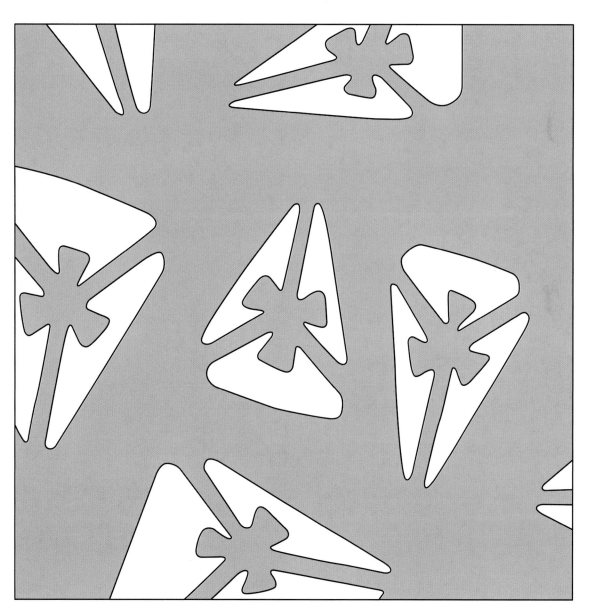

Master Stencil 2 (Large): Fruit Interior

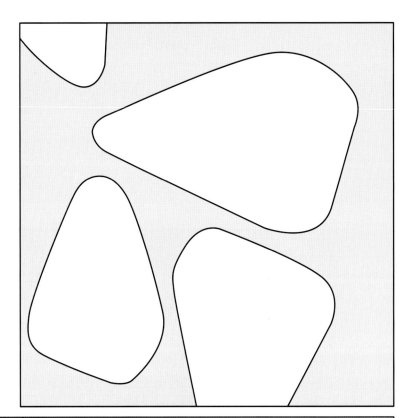

Master Stencil 1 (Small):
Fruit Exterior

Master Stencil 1 (Medium):
Fruit Exterior

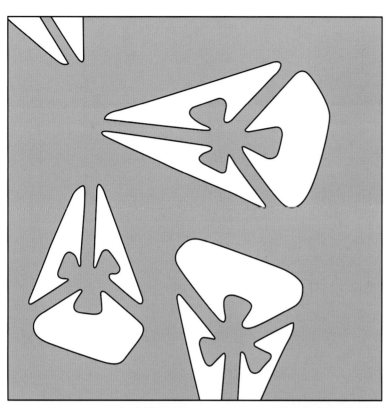

Master Stencil 2 (Small):
Fruit Interior

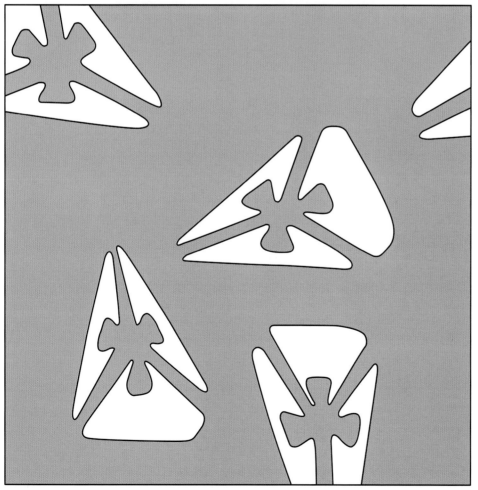

Master Stencil 2 (Medium):
Fruit Interior

Festive Holiday Ornament Trio

Every December, my husband, daughter, and I each make a handmade ornament for our holiday tree. My medium of choice—surprise!—is paper. Here's my paper-cut take on three traditional winter holiday icons. Beginners can make quick work of the crescent shapes and simple stovepipe hat for this Jaunty Snowman. And while the Botanical Snowflake is geared towards advanced cutters, it's just more

complex shapes repeated to form a circle. Practice those tight corners and you'll have it in time. As a bonus, the Botanical Snowflake is a two-in-one ornament: its interior star cutout forms a Spiral Star pendant. Consider making these in multiples and presenting them as handmade gifts, or using them to create a pattern or theme on your holiday tree.

CARDSTOCK CUTTING LIST

Jaunty Snowman

- Any color cardstock (master stencils 1 and 2): (2) 4" x 5" (100 x 130mm)
- Any color cardstock (master stencil 3): (1) 2" x 3" (50 x 75mm)
- Pale blue cardstock (top layer): 4" x 5" (100 x 130mm) square
- Royal blue cardstock (bottom layer): 4" x 5" (100 x 130mm) cardstock square
- Black cardstock (hat): 2" x 3" (50 x 75mm) square

Botanical Snowflake
SPIRAL STAR BONUS PROJECT MADE FROM BOTANICAL SNOWFLAKE CUTAWAYS

- Any color cardstock (master stencils): (2) 6" x 6" (150 x 150mm)
- Rainforest green cardstock (top layer, snowflake; middle layer, star): 6" x 6" (150 x 150mm) square
- Creamy white cardstock (middle layer, snowflake; top layer, star): 6" x 6" (150 x 150mm) square
- Crimson red cardstock (bottom layer, snowflake; bottom layer, star): 6" x 6" (150 x 150mm) square

TOOLS AND MATERIALS

- ⅛" (3mm) or 1⁄16" (2mm) hand-held circular punch (see Resources, p. 142)
- Linen thread or jute string
- Self-healing cutting mat
- Metal ruler
- Craft knife, such as X-ACTO knife
- Blades for craft knife, such as X-ACTO #11 blades
- 2B pencil
- Adhesive pick-up square
- Liquid adhesive for paper

Holiday ornament trio for modern holidays. The Jaunty Snowman's bulb shapes are a variation on a classic Chinese lantern paper-cutting design and the Botanical Snowflake was inspired by a Karl Blossfeldt flower photograph. All three pendants' color combinations reflect my eclectic household traditions.

PHOTO BY LISA FRANCHOT

Jaunty Snowman

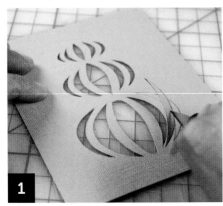

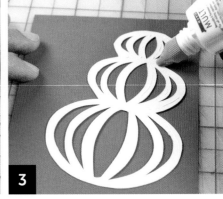

1

2

3

Prepare the Jaunty Snowman master stencils. Trim the cardstock to the specifications shown on the cutting list. Photocopy and transfer the designs to cardstock. For the interior master stencil, cut the inner crescents first, then work toward the right and left crescents. Mark the interior "Master Stencil 1," the silhouette "Master Stencil 2," and the hat "Master Stencil 3."

Cut the pale blue layer. Place Master Stencil 1 on the pale blue cardstock, pencil the design in, and cut out the crescent shapes as directed in Step 1. Align Master Stencil 2 on the cardstock, making sure that the silhouette rests evenly around the crescent shapes you just cut. Pencil in the design and cut out the silhouette.

Adhere the pale blue and royal blue layers. Lightly dot glue on the entire back surface of the snowman's body. Be sure there is at least 1" (25mm) of royal blue paper around the body. Then adhere the pale blue shape to the royal blue paper and burnish.

Cut the royal blue layer. On the darker blue paper, sketch an approximately ¹⁄₁₆" (2mm)-wide border around the pale blue snowman silhouette, making sure it follows the stacked ovals' curvature. Cut along the sketch line and lift out the now two-layer snowman from the paper.

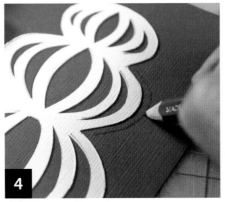

4

5

Stencil, cut out, and attach the hat. Place Master Stencil 3 on black cardstock, pencil in the shape, and cut it out. Position the hat on the snowman's head at a pleasing angle. Pencil the hat's position on the snowman, and apply glue only within that area. Reposition and adhere the hat to the snowman and burnish.

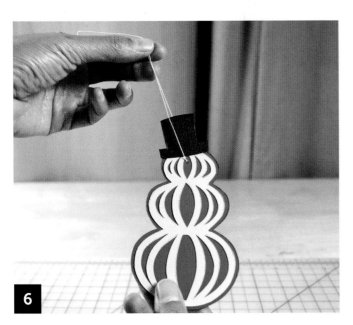

6

Create a hanger. Punch a hole about ¼" (6mm) from the top of the snowman's head using a hand-held circular punch. Cut 8" (205mm) of linen thread, insert it through the hole, and tie it into a knot to form a loop. Trim off any excess thread on either side of the knot. Finally, use a "dab and pull" motion to erase any remaining glue or pencil marks with an adhesive pick-up square.

Botanical Snowflake

1

Prepare the master stencils. Photocopy and transfer the designs to any color cardstock. On both stencils, include the 1" (25mm) border and the N, S, E, and W letters, which will help you locate the top of the design. Cut out the fork shapes first, followed by the star shape. Mark the interior stencil "Master Stencil 1" and the exterior one "Master Stencil 2."

2

Cut the green layer. Place Master Stencil 1 on the green cardstock, stencil the design, and trim out the shapes using the same order of cuts as Step 1. With the Master Stencil in place, lightly mark N, S, E, and W on the green layer. Set aside the interior green starburst cutout for later. Align Master Stencil 2 atop the design with N, S, E, and W in their proper orientation. Master Stencil 2 should rest evenly around the interior shapes. Pencil in the design and trim out the silhouette.

3

Adhere the green and white layers. Apply very thin dotted lines of glue to the green snowflake. (Dip a toothpick in glue if necessary.) Be sure to cover all of the corners. Lay the snowflake atop the white cardstock and burnish. Lightly draw a ½" (1mm)-wide white border that follows the curvature of the green snowflake on both the outside and the center. Cut the entire shape out. Set the white star aside with the green star you cut earlier.

Adhere the white and red layers. Apply glue to the back of the white layer. Place it atop the red cardstock and burnish.

4

Cut the red layer. Lightly draw a ½₃₂" (1mm)-wide red border that follows the curvature of the snowflake's white border. Cut along the sketch lines and pop out the final snowflake.

Create a hanger. About ¼" (6mm) from the top of one of the snowflake's fork shapes, punch a tiny hole. Cut 8" (205mm) of linen thread, insert it into the hole, and knot it to form a hanging loop. Trim off any excess thread on either side of the knot. Finally, use a "dab and pull" motion to erase all pencil marks and dried glue with an adhesive pick-up square.

tip: PROTECT THIN SHAPES

As you trim the outer edge of the snowflake in Step 2, you will create thin, filigreed shapes. To prevent tearing, use your non-cutting hand's fingertips to anchor the paper for stability. Cut sharp corners so that the snowflake detaches easily from the paper.

Bonus Ornament: Spiral Star

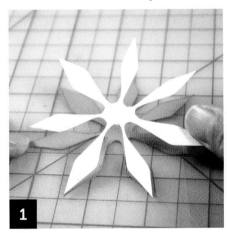

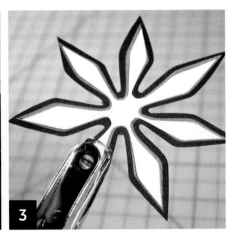

Glue the white and green stars. Position the cutaway white starburst shape inside the green star shape. Glue the two together and burnish.

Add a red border. Glue the green and white star to leftover red cardstock. Lightly draw a ½₃₂" (1mm) red border and trim out the final star.

Attach a loop hole. Punch a hole in one of the star's rays. Loop a 6" (150mm) thread through the hole and tie a knot. Trim off any excess thread on either side of the knot.

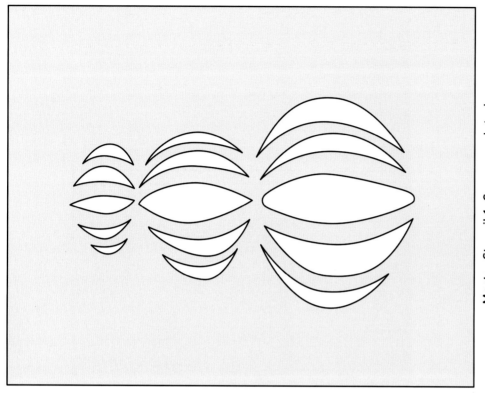

Master Stencil 1: Snowman Interior
Be sure to use this stencil first, and then use Master Stencil 2.

Master Stencil 3:
Snowman Hat

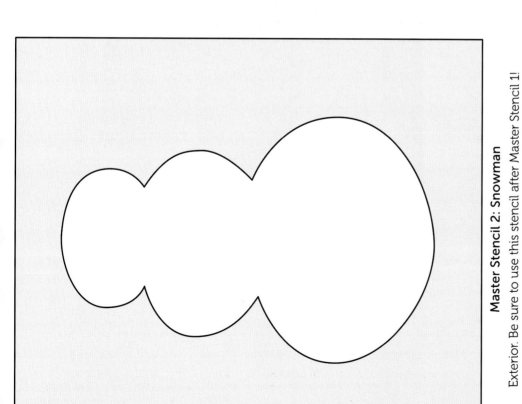

Master Stencil 2: Snowman
Exterior. Be sure to use this stencil after Master Stencil 1!

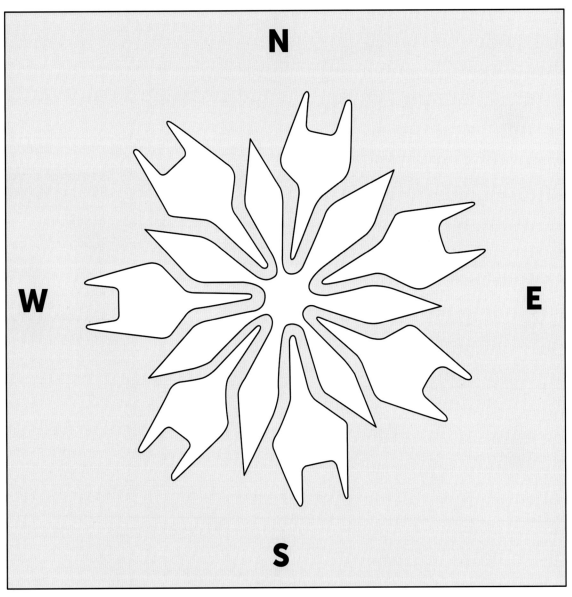

Master Stencil 1: Snowflake Interior
Be sure to use this stencil first, and then use Master Stencil 2.

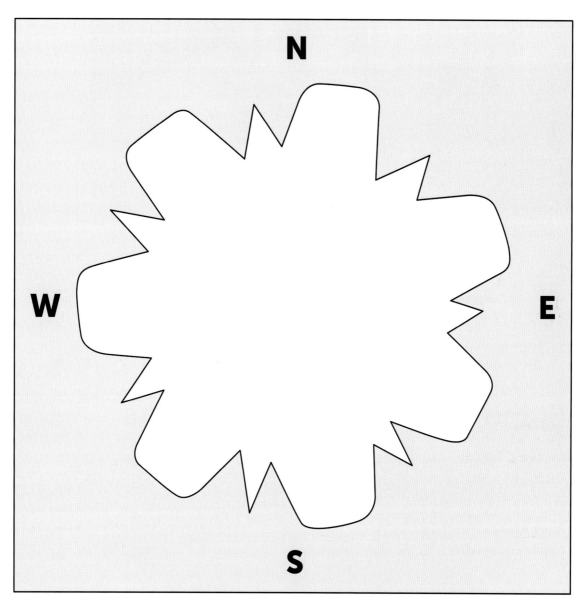

Master Stencil 2: Snowflake Exterior
Be sure to use this stencil after Master Stencil 1!

PHOTO BY LISA FRANCHOT

Stand-Alone Decorative Frame

Though I enjoy sharing digital photos, when it comes to keepsakes, nothing replaces an artfully framed photo print. I stumbled upon self-adhesive easel backs at the art store, which inspired me to design a frame entirely from paper. I cut an Arts & Crafts-style decorative mat, hinged it to a backing, and attached an easel back. The easel folds flat, so it's easy to tuck the piece into an 8" x 10" (205 x 255mm) envelope as a spectacular photo greeting card. It also makes a memorable handmade gift for bridesmaids, grandparents, or teachers.

Decorative Frame: Surprising Stems. I tend to take familiar images and add unexpected touches as I did with this Flower Geometry pattern. Here, the stems get as much attention as the flower bulbs to form a lovely grid. Sleek bulbs and sharp triangular leaves balance the composition.

CARDSTOCK CUTTING LIST

Any color cardstock (master stencils): 8" x 10" (205 x 255mm) rectangle

- Pale/dove gray cardstock (top layer and frame backing): (2) 8" x 10" (205 x 255mm) rectangles
- Goldenrod yellow (second layer): 8" x 10" (205 x 255mm) rectangle

- Butter yellow cardstock (third layer and flower interiors): 8" x 10" (205 x 255mm) rectangle
- Dark/slate gray cardstock (bottom layer and leaves): 8" x 10" (205 x 255mm) rectangle

TOOLS AND MATERIALS

- Linen book binder's tape, self-adhesive (See Resources, p. 142)
- Cardboard easel back, self-stick: 5" (130mm) for landscape photos, 9" (230mm) for portrait photos
- Removable mounting squares (See Resources, p. 142)
- Self-healing cutting mat

- Metal ruler
- Craft knife, such as X-ACTO knife
- Blades for craft knife, such as X-ACTO #11 blades
- 2B pencil
- Adhesive pick-up square
- Liquid adhesive for paper

1

Prepare the Flower Geometry stencil. Trim the cardstock to the specifications on the cutting list. Photocopy and transfer the design to the 8" x 10" (205 x 255mm) cardstock of any color. Include the interior rectangle. Cut out the shapes, using a ruler to cut the straight, parallel flower stems and the interior rectangle window. Mark this "Master Stencil 1."

2

Cut the pale gray layer. Align Master Stencil 1 atop the light gray 8" x 10" (205 x 255mm) layer. Pencil in the design and cut out the shapes.

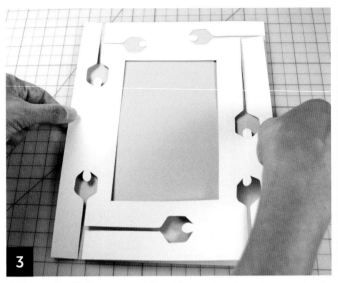

Adhere the light gray and goldenrod yellow layers. Apply glue to the back of the light gray/dove layer. Position it above the goldenrod yellow layer, align the corners, then adhere and burnish.

Draw and trim the flower highlights. On the goldenrod layer, lightly draw the inner half-flower shape (Flower Interior, p. 91). Be sure the shape rests evenly inside the flower bulb. Cut out the seven small shapes.

tip: TRIMMING EXCESS

Each time you glue a new 8" x 10" (205 x 255mm) layer to the previous one, make sure the edges are even by trimming off excess paper if necessary. Align your metal ruler's edge with the top (smaller) layer and trim off the excess paper until all edges are even. (See Technique 9, p. 31, for details.)

Draw and trim the inner photo window. Using your ruler, draw a rectangle about 1/32" (1mm) from each edge of the pale gray photo window. Trim out the goldenrod rectangle.

6

Adhere the goldenrod and butter yellow layers. Apply glue to the back of the goldenrod layer, position it above the butter yellow layer, align the corners, then adhere and burnish.

7

Cut the butter yellow layer. As you did in Steps 1 and 5, cut an inner rectangle about ¹⁄₃₂" (1mm) distance from the goldenrod yellow photo window's edges. The window should now have a three-layer beveled edge. Apply glue to the back of the butter yellow layer, position it above the dark/slate gray 8" x 10" (205 x 255mm) sheet, align the corners, and lay the two pieces together. Burnish.

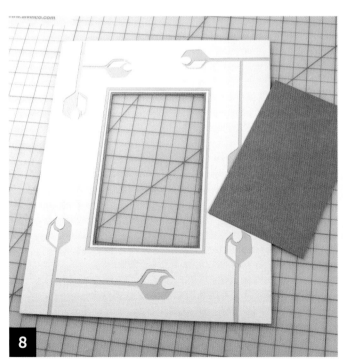

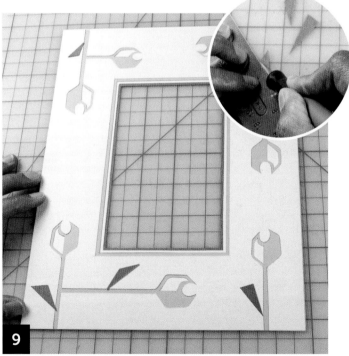

8

Cut out the dark gray/slate photo window. Cut an inner rectangle that is ¹⁄₃₂" (1mm) from the butter yellow photo window's edges. The window should now have a four-layer beveled edge. Set aside the dark gray/slate rectangle cutaway shape for Step 9.

9

Cut and glue the leaves. Trim two ½" x 6" (15 x 150mm) strips from the dark gray/slate cutout rectangle. Angle your ruler sharply between the longer edges of the strips and trim off seven triangles that mimic those in the photograph. Position each cut leaf so that it extends from a flower stem. Glue and burnish.

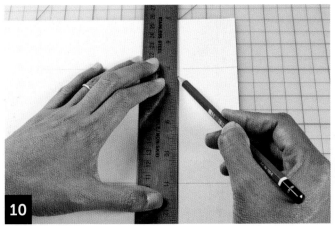

Cut the backing. On the remaining sheet of light gray/dove 8" x 10" (205 x 255mm) cardstock, draw four lines that are 2" (50mm) from each edge, forming a 4" x 6" (100 x 150mm) rectangle in the center.

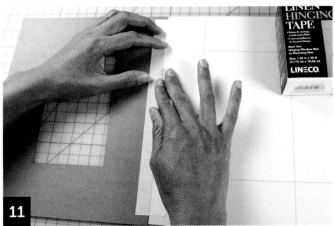

Hinge the photo frame and backing. Lay the four-layer piece next to the backing you just cut. Be sure both are in portrait orientation, flush but not overlapping, with back sides facing up. Cut a 9½" (240mm) length of self-adhesive linen bookbinder's tape. Peel the tape backing and form a hinge by resting one half of the tape on each rectangle. Burnish and fold.

Secure the photo. Attach removable mounting squares to your photo's corners and adhere to the backing. Check the photo's placement by folding the mat over the image. Reposition the photo if necessary.

Seal the frame and attach the easel. Place a removable mounting square on the two unhinged corners of the frame's mat. Fold over and burnish the mat and photo backing. Draw a line to mark the bottom midway point of the 8" (205mm) edge (if your photo is in portrait orientation) or the middle of the 10" (255mm) edge (if the photo is in landscape orientation). Peel the easel's adhesive backing, align the easel with the line you drew, and adhere it to the photo frame.

tip: PLACING THE EASEL

Be sure the bottom of the easel is ever so slightly above the edge of the frame so that there is room for the frame to lean at a slight angle.

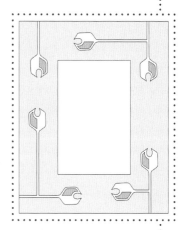

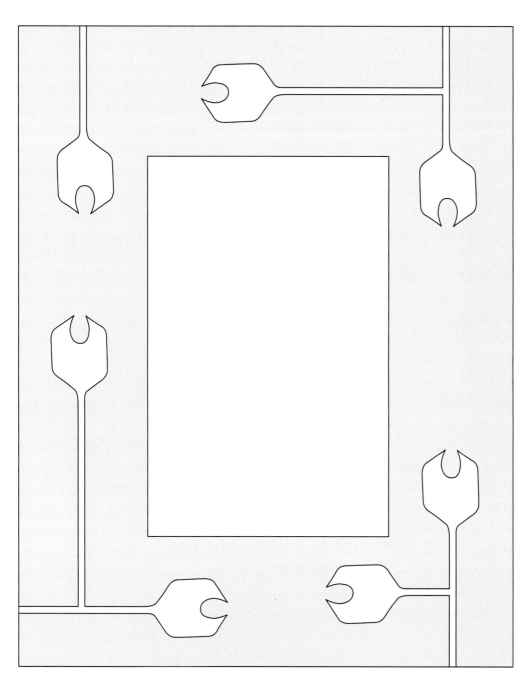

Master Stencil 1: Flower Geometry Frame
Copy at 150%

x7

Illustration:
Flower Interior

You Can Also Try:

Using It as a Photo Mat
Skip Step 13 and simply insert the mat into an elegant wood 8" x 10" (205 x 255mm) frame of your choice.

Hanging It Up
Skip Step 13 and attach the matted frame to a wall with removable putty or removable hanging strips. See Resources, page 142.

chapter 3

Wall Art

* * * * * * * * * * * * * * * * * *

For kids' or adults' rooms, these modern, graphic pieces are an

eye-catching alternative to paintings or photography. The designs

go straight from cutting mat to frame with satisfying speed and

for not much more than the cost of cardstock. Though I give you

specific color combinations, feel free to experiment to find the

right color choices for any room.

Kids' Monogram Wall Art, page 94
PHOTO BY LISA FRANCHOT.

PHOTO BY LISA FRANCHOT

Kids' Monogram Wall Art

As a new mom, I received lovely gifts that helped welcome my daughter into the world. So when my friends became parents, I wanted to pay that joy forward with a handmade gift that would stand the test of time. Thus were born these wall art squares with vibrant, retro-modern car and heart designs that hang well in any nursery. Personalize them with a child's initial by adding a letter. Each finished piece fits easily inside a 6" x 6" (150 x 150mm) frame. Be prepared to make these more than once—for all the new parents in your life, or your own children's rooms.

Kids' Wall Art: Classic and Modern at Once. My parents' baby blue VW "Bug" was the inspiration for this retro modern Bumper-to-Bumper pattern. The Modern Hearts pattern takes an iconic motif and adds Mid-Century Modern flair. Both bring graphic cheer to any kids' room.

CARDSTOCK CUTTING LIST

Bumper-to-Bumper

- Any color cardstock (master stencils): (2) 6" x 6" (150 x 150mm) squares
- Yam orange cardstock (top layer): 6" x 6" (150 x 150mm) square
- Butter yellow cardstock (middle layer): 6" x 6" (150 x 150mm) square
- Royal blue cardstock (bottom layer and letter): 6" x 6" (150 x 150mm) square

Modern Hearts

- Any color cardstock (master stencils): (2) 6" x 6" (150 x 150mm) squares
- Crimson red cardstock (top layer): 6" x 6" (150 x 150mm) square
- Aqua cardstock (middle layer and letter): 6" x 6" (150 x 150mm) square
- Dark orange cardstock (bottom layer): 6" x 6" (150 x 150mm) square

TOOLS AND MATERIALS

- 6" x 6" (150 x 150mm) wood frame (See Resources, p. 142)
- Self-healing cutting mat
- Metal ruler
- Craft knife, such as X-ACTO knife
- Blades for craft knife, such as X-ACTO #11 blades
- 2B pencil
- Adhesive pick-up square
- Liquid adhesive for paper

tip: CUTTING CIRCLES

To make circles (the headlights), cut a series of small arcs along the drawn circle while keeping the knife blade lodged in the paper. Rotate the paper clockwise after you cut each arc until you return to the starting point. If you leave any divots, shave them off by repositioning the blade just to the right or left of each divot and pull the knife along the curvature to remove.

Bumper-to-Bumper

1

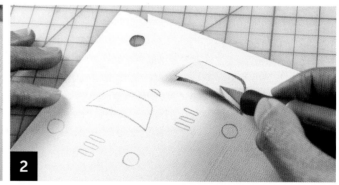

2

Prepare the car body master stencil. Trim the cardstock to the specifications shown on the cutting list. Photocopy and transfer the design to a 6" x 6" (150 x 150mm) square of any color. Cut out the shapes and mark this "Master Stencil 1."

Prepare the windshield and grill master stencil. Photocopy and transfer the design to a 6" x 6" (150 x 150mm) square of any color. Cut out the shapes and mark this "Master Stencil 2."

Bumper-to-Bumper, continued

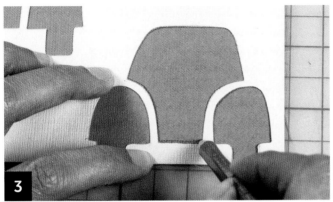

Cut the orange layer. Align Master Stencil 1 atop the orange rectangle, draw in the design, and cut out the shapes.

Adhere the orange and yellow layers. Lightly apply glue to the back of the orange layer. Align the orange and yellow layers, adhere, and burnish.

Cut the yellow layer. Align Master Stencil 2 atop the two-ply orange/yellow sheet. Lightly draw in the design. Be sure the windshield, grill, and headlight shapes are spaced properly inside each car. Erase and redraw any shapes that fell out of registration, then cut out all of the shapes.

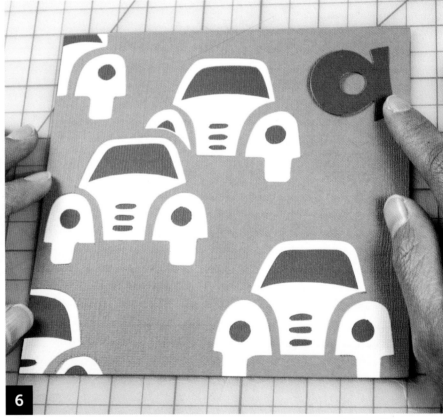

Adhere the yellow and blue layers. Apply glue to the back of the yellow square. Position it above the blue square and align the corners. Adhere and burnish. Design and sketch the letter of the child's first name approximately 1½" wide and 2" tall (40 x 50mm) on royal blue cardstock. Trim it out and adhere it to the top right corner. Use the adhesive pick-up square to dab and pull at any remaining pencil marks and dried glue. Place inside the frame and hang.

Modern Hearts

Prepare the outer hearts master stencil. Trim the cardstock to the specifications shown on the cutting list. Photocopy and transfer the pattern to the 6" x 6" (150 x 150mm) cardstock. Cut out the shapes and mark this "Master Stencil 1."

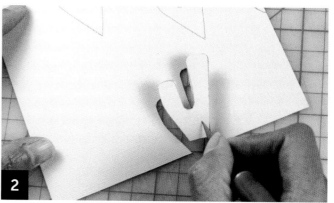

Prepare the inner hearts master stencil. Photocopy and transfer the pattern to 6" x 6" (150 x 150mm) cardstock of any color. Cut out the shapes and mark this "Master Stencil 2."

Cut the red layer and adhere the red and aqua layers. Align Master Stencil 1 atop the red 6" x 6" (150 x 150mm) square, draw in the design, and cut out the shapes. Lightly apply glue to the back of the red layer. Align the red and aqua layers, adhere, and burnish.

Cut the aqua layer. Align Master Stencil 2 atop the two-ply red/aqua square. Lightly draw in the design. Be sure the inner heart shapes you drew are spaced properly inside the red hearts. Erase and redraw any that fell out of registration and cut out all the shapes.

Adhere the aqua and orange layers. Apply glue to the back of the aqua layer. Position it above the orange square, align the corners, adhere, and burnish.

Add an initial and complete the project. Design and sketch a child's initial approximately 1½" wide and 2" tall (40 x 50mm) on aqua cardstock. Trim the letter out and adhere it to the middle right side. Use the adhesive pick-up square to dab and pull at any remaining pencil marks and dried glue. Place inside the frame and hang.

Master Stencil 1: Car Body

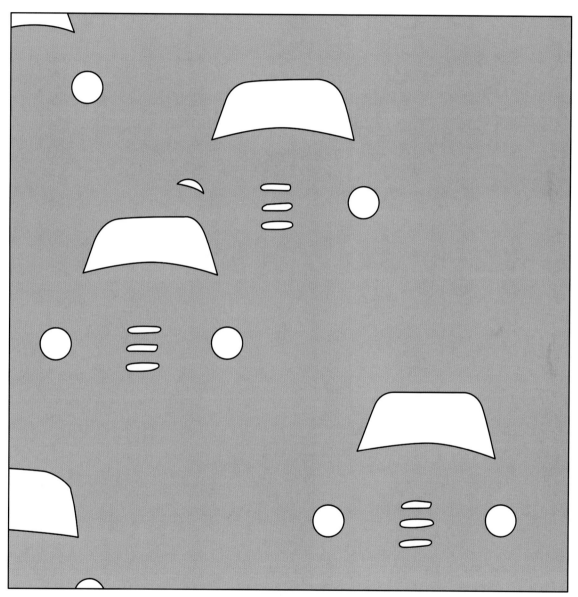

Master Stencil 2: Windshield and Grill

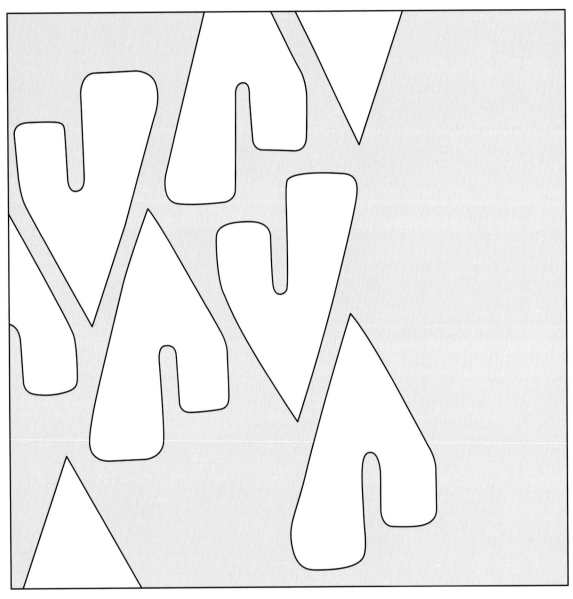

Master Stencil 1: Outer Hearts

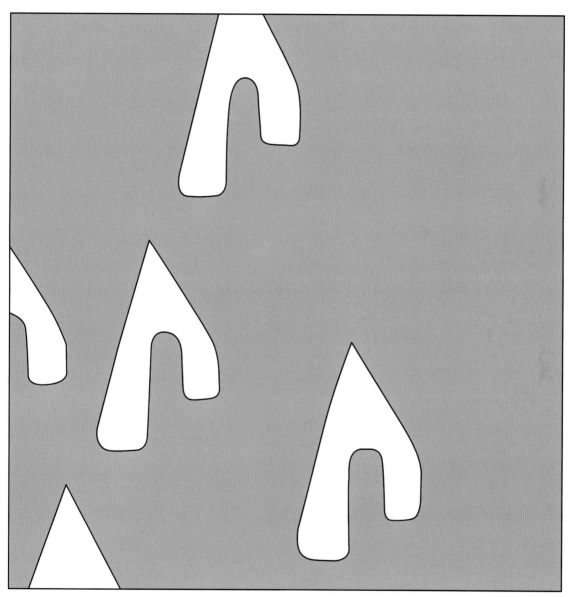

Master Stencil 2: Inner Hearts

You Can Also Try:

Completing a Full Monogram Trio

Use the master stencils to recreate the car or heart pattern two or three times, one for each initial of the child's monogram. Frame and hang two or three squares left to right, spaced closely together or stacked top to bottom.

Ordering a Shadow Box Frame

Ask a professional framer to create a shadow box frame for your wall art. The extra space between the paper art and the glass accentuates the paper's layers.

Spiral Flower Triptych

Because I have a thing for designing in threes, I keep a stash of inexpensive three-window frames in my studio. I created this floral triptych (a Greek term for three-panel art work) just for this type of frame, and I love how they can hang in any room. The project involves one layer of paper cutting, so take your time cutting the petals' slightly rounded outer edges and inner points precisely. You could cut just one 5" x 7" (130 x 180mm) panel and frame it singly, but all three in the same frame make a fantastic study in color's ability to transform a pattern's personality. Note how the petals meet in center points to create a wonderful optical "sparkle."

CARDSTOCK CUTTING LIST

Any color cardstock (master stencil):
5½" x 7½" (140 x 190mm) rectangle

Panel A
- Pale blue cardstock (top layer):
  5½" x 7½" (140 x 190mm) rectangle
- Crimson red cardstock (bottom layer):
  5½" x 7½" (140 x 190mm) rectangle

Panel B
- Yam orange cardstock (top layer):
  5½" x 7½" (140 x 190mm) rectangle
- Royal blue cardstock (bottom layer):
  5½" x 7½" (140 x 190mm) rectangle

Panel C
- Apple green cardstock (top layer):
  5½" x 7½" (140 x 190mm) rectangle
- Navy blue cardstock (bottom layer):
  5½" x 7½" (140 x 190mm) rectangle

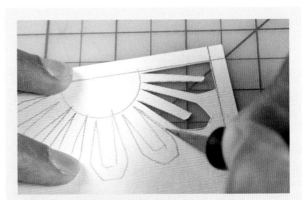

tip: PRESERVING THE SHAPE OF A DESIGN

Each time you transfer this stencil, you're likely to narrow the width of already very slender petals. To preserve the original petal shapes, use a very sharp pencil and cut ever so slightly to the *outside* of the pencil markings.

TOOLS AND MATERIALS

- Wood frame with three-mat window for 5" x 7" (130 x 180mm) images
- Metal ruler
- Craft knife, such as X-ACTO knife
- Blades for craft knife, such as X-ACTO #11 blades
- Artist's tape
- 2B or 3B pencil
- Adhesive pick-up square
- Liquid adhesive for paper
- Self-healing cutting mat

Triptych: Petal Magic. This Blueflower pattern was born when I took a single petal shape and rotated it around a circle. I've been adapting it ever since, refining petal shapes and color combinations. My favorite color ways are shown here.

PHOTO BY LISA FRANCHC

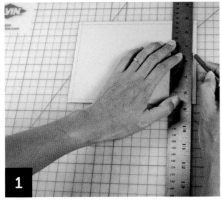

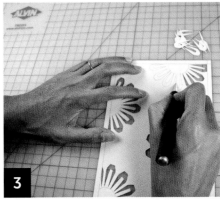

Draw an interior border inside each rectangle. Trim the cardstock to the specifications shown on the cutting list. Measure a ¼" (6mm) border on the pale blue, orange, and green layers, plus the master stencil. Be sure to keep all cuts to the inside of this border to prevent the smaller flower pieces from falling away and make layers easier to glue.

Create the master stencil. Photocopy and transfer the design to the master stencil cardstock. Cut out the petals slowly and methodically, beginning with the inner U of each petal, followed by the outer U. Mark this "Master Stencil."

Cut the top layers. Align the master stencil atop the aqua rectangle. Be sure the ¼" (6mm) pencil border of the stencil and paper beneath it line up as closely as possible. Draw in the design and cut out the shapes. Take care to cut within the ¼" (6 mm) border. Repeat to cut the flower design into the orange and green rectangles.

Adhere the top and bottom layers. Lightly apply glue to the back of the aqua sheet. Line up the corners of the aqua and red paper, lay them together, and burnish. Repeat to adhere the orange layer to the royal blue rectangle and the apple green layer to the navy blue rectangle.

Clean up the art work and display the triptych. Use an adhesive pick-up square to remove pencil marks and dried glue. Mount the artwork with artist's tape to the three-window mat. Be sure the ¼" (6mm) border rests outside the frame windows. Try to avoid placing the art in direct sunlight as the paper colors can fade with time.

tip: KEEPING THE FLOWERS CRISP

To preserve the optical "sparkle" in each flower's center, make sure to cut the petal points so that they line up around an inner concentric circle. To ensure this, after stenciling the flower design, use a 1" (25mm) circle template to lightly draw a smaller inner circle. Then go back with a pencil and extend the petal points so they all lie on this inner circle before you cut out the petals.

Master Stencil: Spiral Flower Triptych

You Can Also Try:

Making Folded Note Cards

Follow the directions through Step 3, and then trim off the entire ¼" (6mm) border. To make the folded note card base (which serves as the bottom layer), cut a 10" x 7" (255 x 180mm) piece of cardstock. Draw a score line halfway along the 10" (255mm) edge and score the piece lengthwise. Fold it in half and crease sharply. Adhere the 5" x 7" (130 x 180mm) flower panel to one of the card's halves. Present in a 5" x 7" (130 x 180mm) envelope.

PHOTO BY LISA FRANCHOT

Arts & Crafts Bunting

As a non-sewer, I never considered making bunting myself until I saw some made of paper. My first effort for my daughter's birthday consisted of nine pennants attached to jute string with hot glue. A little rustic, but its bright patterns transformed the event beautifully. Best of all, I hung the piece in her room afterward as wall art! With a few tweaks and just one master stencil, I came up with this better

version: six pennants featuring a winding leaf design, plus four additional pennants crafted from the leftover cutaway shapes. All ten flags are secured by folding the final paper layer—a diamond that splits into two triangles—over chic linen piping. Hang this versatile bunting at weddings, showers, graduations, or other elegant functions.

Arts and Crafts Bunting: Winning Pennants. An Arts and Crafts Movement fan, I created this Winding Leaf pattern for my very first holiday card and adapted it here using just three colors in three combinations. They're versatile enough to make any room a celebratory one.

CARDSTOCK CUTTING LIST

Any color cardstock (master stencil): 6" x 6" (305 x 305mm) square

- Butter yellow cardstock (thin triangles, full triangles, base diamonds, and leaf design): (2) 12" x 12" (305 x 305mm) squares
- Forest green cardstock (thin triangles, full triangles, base diamonds, and leaf design): (2) 12" x 12" (305 x 305mm) squares

- Sky blue cardstock (thin triangles, full triangles, base diamonds, and leaf design): (2) 12" x 12" (305 x 305mm) squares
- Tan/beige cardstock (base diamonds): (2) 12" x 12" (305 x 305mm) squares

TOOLS AND MATERIALS

- 4 yards (4m) of ½" (13mm) ribbon or piping
- Fabric glue (or liquid glue)
- Self-healing cutting mat
- Metal ruler
- Craft knife, such as X-ACTO knife

- Blades for craft knife, such as X-ACTO #11 blades
- 2B pencil
- Adhesive pick-up square
- Liquid adhesive for paper

Winding Leaf Pennants Layout

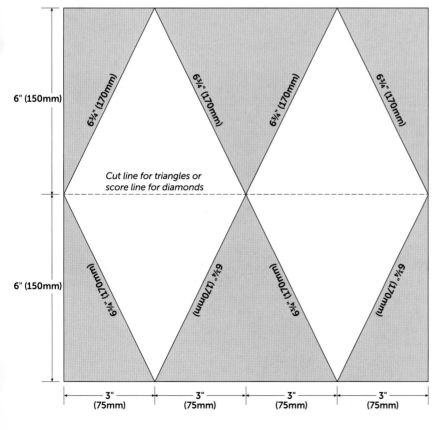

1

Trim the triangle layers. Lightly draw lines on the back of the yellow 12" x 12" (305 x 305mm) cardstock according to the illustration at left. You should have a total of four triangles with bases of 6" (150mm) each in the center of the cardstock. Trim out the center four triangles. Set aside the thinner triangle cutaways for later. Repeat this drawing and cutting process with the blue and green 12" x 12" (305 x 305mm) sheets for a total of 10 triangle bases.

note: WHY DIAMONDS?

You will use the same diagram to cut diamonds and triangles. The diamond is composed of two triangles joined at the base. When scored and folded, the four diamonds will form the triangular base layer of each pennant.

Trim the diamond base layers.
You will now measure and cut the following: two yellow diamonds, two blue diamonds, two green diamonds, and four tan diamonds. To start, lightly pencil lines according to the illustration (Step 1) on the back of a yellow 12" x 12" (305 x 305mm) sheet. This time, instead of trimming out four triangles, trim out the center two diamonds; each diamond should have four sides measuring 6¾" (170mm) each plus a 6" (150mm) score line in the center. Set aside the leftover thin triangle cutaways for later. Repeat this process with one blue, one green, and two tan 12" x 12" (305 x 305mm) sheets.

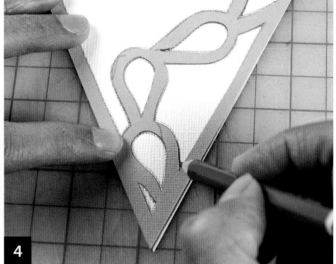

Prepare the Winding Leaves master stencil. Cut a 6" x 6" (150 x 150mm) any color cardstock square. Mark a dot halfway (3" or 76mm) across one of the edges, then draw a triangle by connecting that dot to the two opposite corners of the square. Cut out the triangle. Photocopy and transfer the Winding Leaf stencil to the triangle. Cut the teardrop-shaped leaves first, followed by the other shapes. Mark this "Master Stencil."

Cut six top layers. Align the master stencil atop a yellow triangle. Draw in the design and cut out the shapes as you did in Step 3. Repeat this stenciling process five more times until you have two yellow, two green, and two blue pennants with Winding Leaf cutouts.

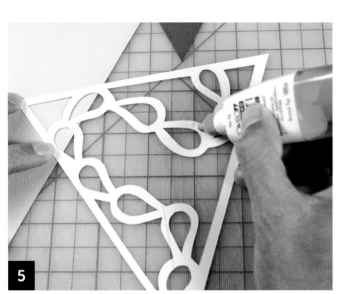

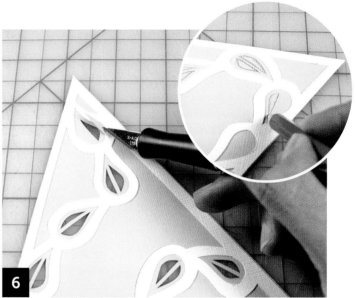

Adhere the first and second layers. Apply glue to the back of a cut yellow triangle. Align it above an uncut blue triangle, adhere, and burnish. Repeat this process until each cut triangle is adhered to a second layer in a color other than its own. You should be left with six different pennants in color combinations of blue, yellow, and green.

Draw and cut the inner split leaf shape. Using the split leaf illustration (p. 111) as a guide, sketch two leaf halves nested inside each teardrop shaped leaf of each pennant. Cut these out.

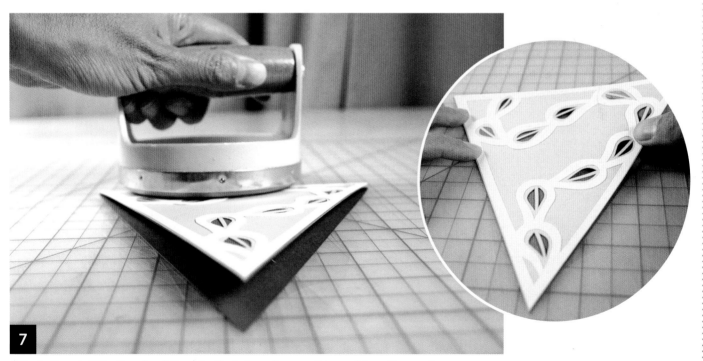

Attach the six Winding Leaf flags to their base layers. Score all ten diamonds and fold them in half. Lay each two-ply triangle completed in Steps 1-6 onto the diamond whose color it lacks. For example, if the top two layers are yellow and blue, adhere it to a green diamond. If the top two layers are blue and green, glue it to the yellow diamond, and so on.

Bi-Color Pennants

Finish the remaining four flags.
Using the thin cutaway triangles left over from Steps 1 and 2 in the Winding Leaf flag, lay two thin triangles atop a tan diamond to form a bi-color flag. Combine green and yellow, yellow and blue, and/or yellow and green half triangles to form four pennants. Apply glue and attach to a folded beige diamond. Burnish.

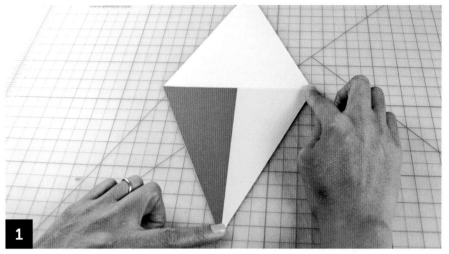

Assemble the Pennants

Attach the flags to the ribbon.
Beginning 30" (1m) from the left end of the ribbon or piping, adhere the pennants in the following pattern: one bi-color pennant followed by two Winding Leaf pennants (and ending with one bi-color pennant at the right). Leave 2" (50mm) between each flag. Apply a thin line of glue just below the score line of the first pennant. Lay the ribbon piping flat atop the glue and allow the glue to set for a minute or two. Weight each pennant with a book to flatten if necessary. There should be about 30" (1m) of ribbon on the right end.

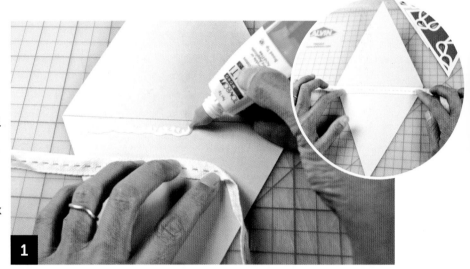

Seal each pennant. Apply glue to the pennant's unsealed edges and fold over. Burnish. Repeat this for each pennant.

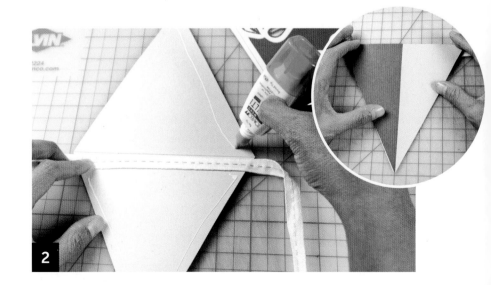

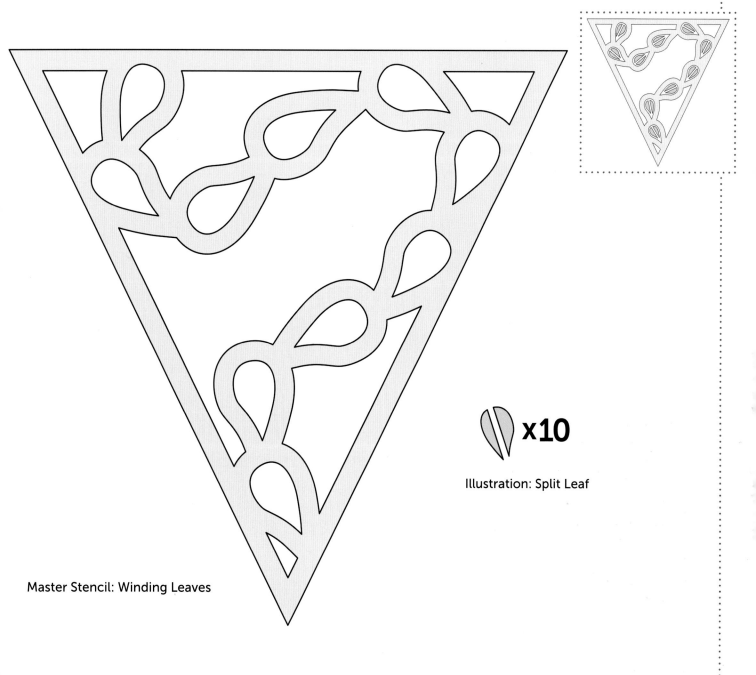

x10

Illustration: Split Leaf

Master Stencil: Winding Leaves

You Can Also Try:

Making Longer Bunting
You should have enough thin triangles to create quite a few more pennants. Create more diamond base pennants as you did in Step 2 (p. 108) and affix the thin triangles to them. To calculate how much ribbon to buy, allow 30" (1m) for right and left ends, 6" (150mm) per pennant, and 2" (50mm) in between each pennant.

Adding a Name or Message
Cut your own alphabet letters to spell out the name(s) of the person being celebrated or the appropriate message ("Welcome Home," "Cheers," "Celebrate").

Using It As Wall Art After the Party
You worked too hard on the bunting to toss it! Spray each pennant with Acrylic Spray Sealant (see Resources, p. 142) and hang it permanently in a child's bedroom or other room of your choice.

Stationery

* * * * * * * * * * * * * * * * *

To my mind, stationery is meant to set off the beauty of the written

word with a visual punch. These four projects do so—with the

added tactile appeal created by layered paper. Try making the gift

card holder and wine tags in batches (like cookies!) and stash a

few note card folios and covered journals as go-to gifts. Most can

be recycled and framed as wall art.

Mid-Century Modern Stationery Set, page 132
PHOTO BY LISA FRANCHOT.

Happy Hour Wine Tag

Get ready to wow the party host when you present your wine bottle with this brightly layered hanging gift tag. The wine glass pattern is relatively easy to cut, so make and keep a stash of them handy for holidays or hostess gifts. They slip right over a bottle's neck and have a built-in space for your handwritten message. It's easy to alter these color trios to suit any season, holiday, or color palette.

CARDSTOCK CUTTING LIST

Any color cardstock (master stencils): (2) 3½" x 7" (90 x 180mm) rectangles

Tag 1

- Crimson red cardstock (top layer): 3½" x 7" (90 x 180mm) rectangle
- Butter yellow cardstock (middle layer): 3½" x 9" (90 x 230mm) rectangle
- Aqua cardstock (bottom layer): 3½" x 7" (90 x 180mm) rectangle

Tag 2

- Grass green cardstock (top layer): 3½" x 7" (90 x 180mm) rectangle
- Palest green cardstock (middle layer): 3½" x 9" (90 x 230mm) rectangle
- Deep purple cardstock (bottom layer): 3½" x 7" (90 x 180mm) rectangle

TOOLS AND MATERIALS

- Combo circle template (See Resources, p. 142)
- ¼" (6mm)-radius corner rounder (See Resources, p. 142)
- Self-healing cutting mat
- Metal ruler
- Craft knife, such as X-ACTO knife
- Blades for craft knife, such as X-ACTO #11 blades
- 2B pencil
- Adhesive pick-up square
- Liquid adhesive for paper

 Wine Tag: Cheers to Entertaining. To create a wine hang tag that delivered my gift message with flair, I cut this pattern with my favorite wine glass silhouette turned on its side for a playful touch.

With love and thanks
from Anna B.
Congratulations!
You did it!
All the best,
Anna

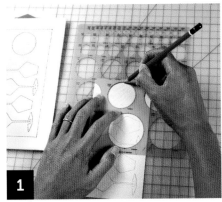

1

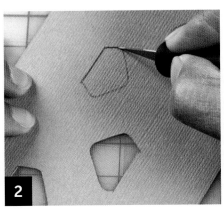

2

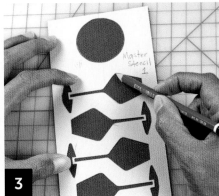

3

Prepare the wine glass master stencil. Trim the cardstock to the specifications shown on the cutting list. Photocopy and transfer the design to a 3½" x 7" (90 x 180mm) cardstock rectangle of any color. Use the combo circle template's 1⅝" (40mm)-diameter circle to trace the circle for the bottle neck. Cut out the shapes and mark this "Master Stencil 1."

Prepare the wine levels master stencil. Photocopy and transfer this design to a 3½" x 7" (90 x 180mm) cardstock rectangle of any color. Use the 1½" (40mm)-diameter circle to trace the inner bottle neck circle. Cut out the shapes and mark this "Master Stencil 2."

Cut the red layer. Align Master Stencil 1 atop the red rectangle, draw in the design, and cut out the shapes.

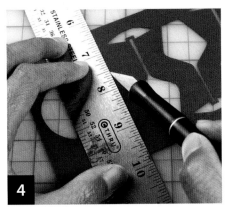

4

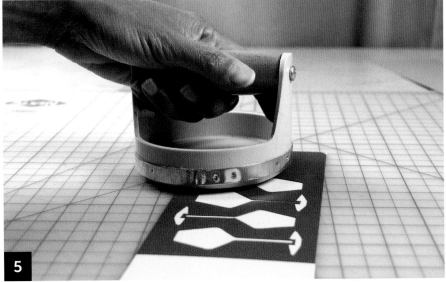

5

Score the red layer's flap. Measure 2" (50mm) from the top edge of the back/untextured side and pencil in a score line (it should rest just beneath the circle). Use the dull side of the craft knife to score the line, creating a 2" (50mm) flap. Crease the line to fold the flap. Use the corner rounder to round the top two corners of the red layer.

Adhere the red and yellow layers. Apply glue to the back of the red layer. Align the top right and left corners of the red and yellow sheets and burnish. The yellow layer should extend 2" (50mm) below the red layer.

tip: CUTTING CIRCLES

Don't worry about cutting a precisely perfect circle. Start at one point in the circle and use your non-cutting hand to rotate the paper in small, evenly spaced arcs as you move the blade along the drawing path.

6 Stencil and cut the yellow layer. Align Master Stencil 2 atop the red-yellow layered piece, draw in the wine levels and inner circle, and cut out the shapes. Use the corner punch to round all four corners of the red-yellow layer.

7 Score the yellow layer's flap. Measure 2" (50mm) from the top edge on the back side and pencil in a score line (it should rest just beneath the circle). Use the dull side of the craft knife to score a 2" (50mm) flap. Crease the flap to fold it.

8 Adhere the yellow and aqua layers. Apply glue to the back of the yellow sheet below the score line only. Line up one of the aqua rectangle's 3½" (90mm) edges with the yellow layer's scored line. Lay the yellow and aqua sheets together and burnish.

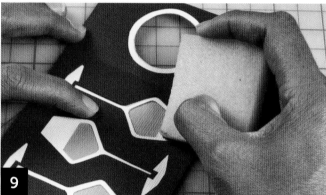

9 Finish the tag. Remove pencil marks and glue. Then fold the top of the gift tag along the score line. Repeat the process for the second tag's color way, substituting dark green, pale green, and dark purple layers for red, yellow, and aqua. Write your message on the bottom space, hang the tag over the bottle neck and present it.

You Can Also Try:

Altering the Design
Change the color trio or make all of the wine levels in Master Stencil 2 the same height. For color combinations I recommend the order layer: dark, light, dark.

'Recycling' the Glasses
Save the wine glass cutouts and use them to decorate place cards. Measure and trim eight 7" x 4" (180 x 100mm) rectangles; score and fold these in half along the 7" (180mm) edge to form table tents. Glue the cutouts on the left of one side of each tent.

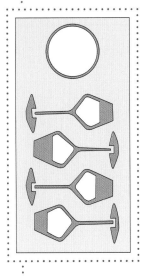

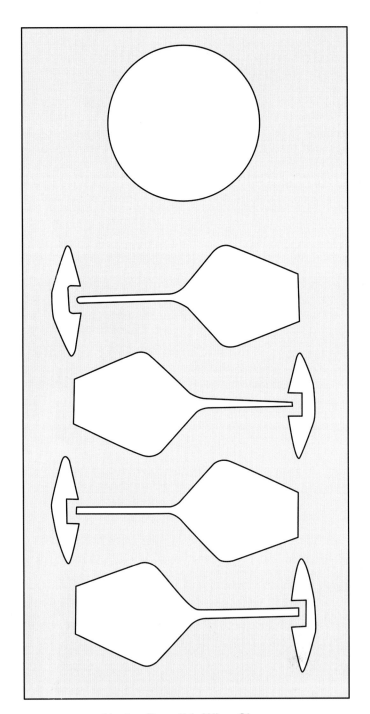

Master Stencil 1: Wine Glass

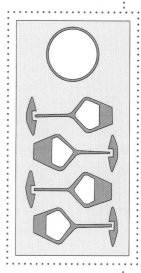

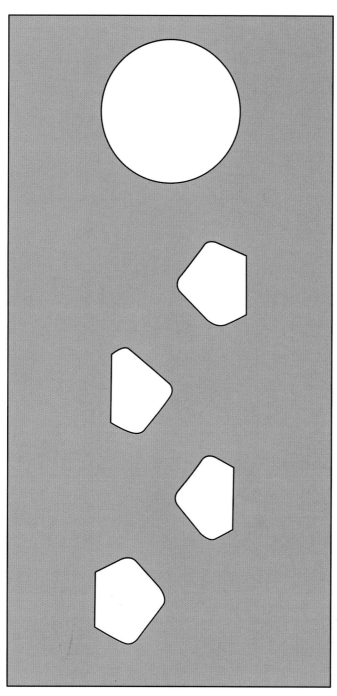

Master Stencil 2: Wine Levels

YIELD: 1 binder

Decorative Recipe Binder

Friends who come for dinner often ask "Can I have the recipe?" but it's hard to find time to make good on that request. One December holiday season, I got organized, photocopied my favorite recipes, and tucked them inside a three-ring kraft binder. To make the gift visually appealing, I placed a bright yellow, purple, and green eggplant pattern on the binder cover.

Friends and family loved the recipes, the organizing tool, and the artwork equally.

Three-ring kraft binders are readily available, and their earthy brown shade goes well with any color combination. I suggest protecting the cover art with coats of Mod Podge, or for a faster process, spraying it with several coats of a water-resistant acrylic sealant.

CARDSTOCK CUTTING LIST

Any color cardstock (eggplant master stencils): (2) 9¾" x 11½" (250 x 290mm) rectangles
Any color cardstock (stem master stencil): 2" x 2" (50 x 50mm) square

- Lemon yellow cardstock (top layer):
  9¾" x 11½" (250 x 290mm) rectangle
- Royal purple cardstock (second layer):
  9¾" x 11½" (250 x 290mm) rectangle
- Lavender cardstock (third layer):
  9¾" x 11½" (250 x 290mm) rectangle

- Cotton candy pink cardstock (bottom layer):
  9¾" x 11½" (250 x 290mm) rectangle
- Deep grass green cardstock (stems):
  6" x 12" (150 x 305mm) rectangle

TOOLS AND MATERIALS

- 100% recycled kraft binder
  (See Resources, p. 142)
- Aerosol acrylic sealant spray
  (See Resources, p. 142) or product such
  as Mod Podge for Paper and sponge
- Self-healing cutting mat
- Metal ruler

- Craft knife, such as X-ACTO knife
- Blades for craft knife, such
  as X-ACTO #11 blades
- 2B pencil
- Adhesive pick-up square
- Liquid adhesive for paper

Recipe Binder: From Classroom to Kitchen. I first cut this Eggplant Trio design along with other vegetable-themed patterns for classroom doors at my daughter's school. The high-contrast purple-yellow-green design transferred easily to this recipe binder, a perfect gift for the home cook.

PHOTO BY LISA FRANCHO

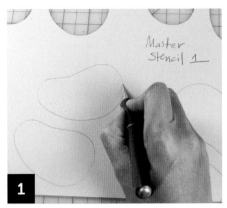

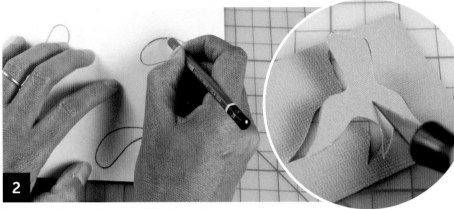

Prepare the eggplant silhouette master stencil. Trim the cardstock to the specifications shown. Photocopy the design at 200% and transfer it to one of the 9¾" x 11½" (250 x 290mm) cardstock rectangles. Cut out the shapes and mark this "Master Stencil 1."

Prepare the teardrop highlight and eggplant stem master stencils. Photocopy the design for the teardrops at 200% and pencil transfer it to one of the 9¾" x 11½" (250 x 290mm) cardstock rectangles. Cut out the shapes and mark this "Master Stencil 2." Photocopy and transfer the stem to the 2" x 2" (50 x 50mm) master stencil cardstock. Cut out the shape and mark this "Master Stencil 3."

Cut the eggplant layer and adhere the yellow and purple layers. Align Master Stencil 1 atop the yellow rectangle, draw in the design, and cut out the shapes. Apply glue to the back of the yellow layer. Line up the corners of the yellow and purple layers, lay them together, and burnish. Trim off any overhanging edges.

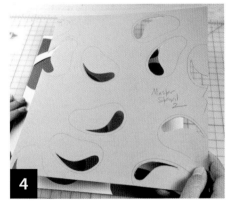

Cut the purple layer. Align Master Stencil 2 atop the two-ply yellow-purple sheet. Pencil in the shapes. Erase and redraw any shapes that fell out of registration, then cut them out.

Adhere the dark purple and lavender layers and cut the interior highlight shape. Apply glue to the back of the purple layer. Line up the corners of the dark purple and lavender layers, lay them together, and burnish. Trim off overhanging edges. On the lavender layer, lightly sketch Final Teardrop shapes (see illustration, p. 125) inside the larger dark purple teardrop shapes. It should be about ⅓ as wide as the larger teardrop. Cut out the lavender shapes.

6

Adhere the lavender and pink layers. Apply glue to the back of the lavender layer. Align it with the pink layer, adhere, and burnish. Trim off any overhanging edges.

7

Cut out and glue the stems. Use Master Stencil 3 to draw eleven stems onto the grass green cardstock. Cut out the shapes, lightly apply glue, and adhere them to the top of the eggplants as shown. Burnish. Some of the stems will hang over the edges of the design. Flip the artwork over so the back side faces up. Locate the overhanging green shapes, place your metal ruler flush with the edge of the pink layer, and carefully trim off the excess green shapes.

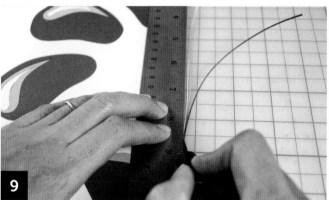

8

Clean up the artwork. Erase all pencil marks and dried glue. Erase from the top of the stem towards the leaf points, not the other way around. If you begin at the points, the eraser can get caught on them, pull up, and rip off the paper.

9

Adhere the finished four-ply design to the binder cover. Check to see that the edges of the artwork line up with those of the binder. If the design is slightly larger than the cover, trim off any overhanging edges. Apply glue to the pink layer, lay atop the binder, and burnish.

tip: SEAL THE BINDER COVER.

Lay the finished artwork atop newspaper or cardboard in a dry, well-ventilated area, preferably outside. Follow directions to spray acrylic sealant in a sweeping motion. Wait until the first coat is dry before applying another. If you're using Mod Podge, take special care to use a sponge applicator and apply it in ultra-thin coats to avoid buckling. Wait until the coat dries completely before re-applying.

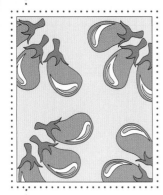

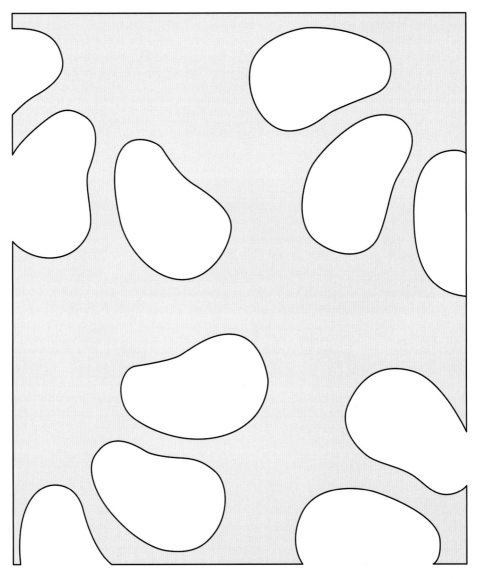

Master Stencil 1: Eggplant Silhouette
Note: Copying this pattern requires the use of oversized paper.
Copy at 200%.

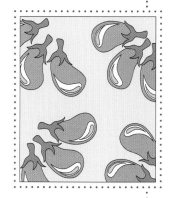

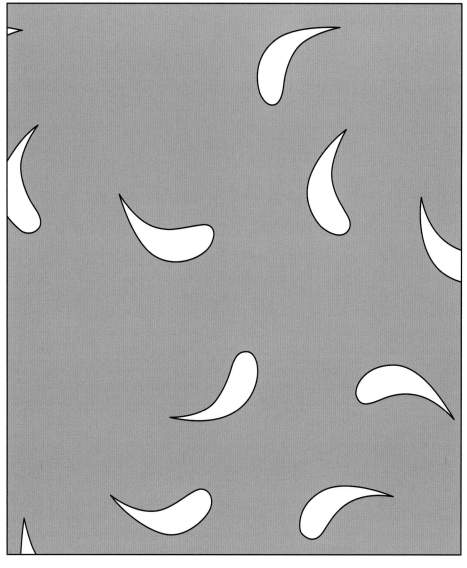

Master Stencil 2: Teardrop Highlight
Copy at 200%.

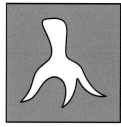

**Master Stencil 3:
Eggplant Stem**
Copy at 200%.

 **x11**

**Illustration:
Final Teardrop**

Gift Card Holder

Gift cards are one of my favorite go-to presents, but it's a challenge to present these plastic cards in a way that both holds the card securely and looks beautiful. My solution? A multi-layered square piece featuring a colorful, elegant pattern on the outside and a simple slit holder inside with plenty of space for a personal note. As a bonus, the piece converts easily to wall art: inserted into a wood 5" x 5" (130 x 130mm) frame, it hangs in style for years to come.

CARDSTOCK CUTTING LIST

Any color cardstock (master stencils): (2) 5" x 5" (130 x 130mm) squares

- Purple-gray cardstock (top layer): 5" x 5" (130 x 130mm) square
- Pale green cardstock (second layer): 5" x 5" (130 x 130mm) square
- Goldenrod yellow cardstock (third layer): 5" x 5" (130 x 130mm) square
- Deep orange cardstock (bottom layer): 5" x 10" (130 x 255mm) square

TOOLS AND MATERIALS

- Standard 3½" x 2⅛" (90 x 55mm) gift card
- 5" x 5" (130 x 130mm) frame (optional)
- Self-healing cutting mat
- Metal ruler
- Craft knife, such as X-ACTO knife
- Blades for craft knife, such as X-ACTO #11 blades
- 2B pencil
- Adhesive pick-up square
- Liquid adhesive for paper

Gift Card Holder: Stylized Wings. Try nestling a gift card in this warm, bright, wing pattern. Its purple and bright orange motif is my interpretation of the beauty of birds' upper and lower wing feathers.

Cover Art

1

Prepare the exterior wing master stencil. Trim the cardstock to the specifications shown on the cutting list. Photocopy and transfer the exterior wing design to the 5" x 5" (130 x 130mm) cardstock of any color. Cut out the shapes and mark this "Master Stencil 1."

2

Prepare the split wing master stencil. Photocopy and transfer the split wing design to the other 5" x 5" (130 x 130mm) cardstock of any color. Cut out the shapes and mark this "Master Stencil 2."

3

Cut the purple-gray layer. Align Master Stencil 1 atop the purple-gray 5" x 5" (130 x 130mm) layer, draw in the design, and cut out the shapes.

4

Adhere the purple-gray and pale green layers. Apply glue to the back of the purple-gray layer. Align the purple-gray and pale green layers, adhere, and burnish.

5

Cut the pale green layer. Place Master Stencil 2 atop the two-ply purple-green sheet and lightly draw in the design. Be sure the split wing shapes are spaced evenly within the exterior wings. Erase and redraw any shapes that fell out of registration, and cut them out. Round all four corners using a corner punch, if desired.

6

Adhere the pale green and goldenrod layers. Round all four corners of the goldenrod 5" x 5" (130 x 130mm) sheet. Apply glue to the back of the pale green layer. Position it above the goldenrod layer and align the rounded corners. Adhere and burnish.

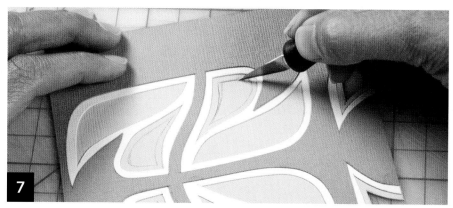

7

Cut the goldenrod layer. Inside the four smallest wing shapes, lightly sketch the Mini Wing shape (see illustration, p. 131) onto the goldenrod layer. Cut the shapes, making sure there is a slim border about 1/32"(1mm) between the yellow and pale green edges.

Gift Card Holder

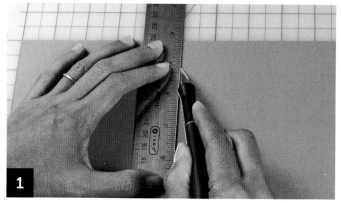

1

2

Score the orange layer. Lay the orange 5" x 10" (130 x 255mm) layer in landscape orientation on your cutting mat. Measure and draw a line midway or 5" (130mm) across the 10" (255mm) edge. Score the line and fold to sharply crease it. With the orange card folded in half, punch all four corners of the square to round them (do only if you have rounded the cover art's corners).

Adhere the cover art and note card. Apply glue to the back of the goldenrod layer. Position it above one half of the orange note card, align the rounded corners, then adhere and burnish with the printing baren.

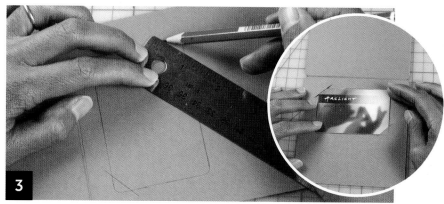

3

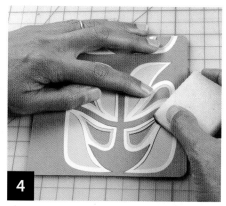

4

Cut the note card slit holders. Lay the gift card within the single-layer orange square (the one without cover art). Trace the gift card's outline with a pencil. Use a ruler to draw 3/4" (20mm) lines diagonally across the top left and bottom right rectangle. Cut slits along these lines and insert a gift card into them.

Clean up your artwork. Remove any pencil marks and dried glue by dabbing and pulling with an adhesive pick-up square.

Master Stencil 1: Exterior Wing

You Can Also Try:

Hanging It

In your personal note, suggest that your recipient remove the gift card and insert the entire piece into a simple wooden 5" x 5" (130 x 130mm) frame. Or purchase the frame yourself (See Resources, p. 142) and include it with your gift card as the "After Party" gift!

Master Stencil 2: Split Wing

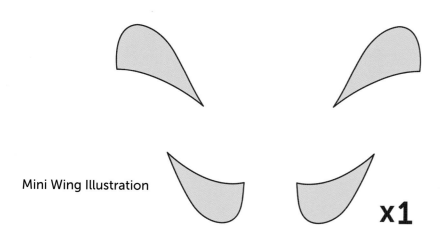

Mini Wing Illustration

x1

Mid-Century Modern Stationery Set

I still remember the first stationery set I received as a child: its matching note cards, envelopes, and stickers were decorated with a wonderful animal pattern and all of the pieces were tucked neatly inside a pocket folder. After I used all of the stationery, I stored my "important" papers inside the folder.

In that spirit, I created this fanciful note card gift set. Follow the directions to create a simple one-pocket folio, and then cut and layer the Duckbill cover art to affix to the folder's cover. Use the duckbill cutouts left over from the cover art to decorate 4" x 6" (100 x 150mm) note cards and tuck them inside the folder. Either pair the note cards with manufactured size A6 envelopes (see Resources, p. 142) or use templates to make the envelopes yourself. The gift set's recipient can even mount the decorative cover art in a 5" x 7" (130 x 150mm) frame after all the notes are sent!

CARDSTOCK CUTTING LIST

Any color cardstock (master stencils): (2) 5" x 8" (130 x 205mm) rectangles

- Butter yellow cardstock (folio):
  10" x 12" (255 x 305mm) rectangle
- Light blue cardstock (top layer, cover art): 5" x 8" (130 x 205mm) rectangle
- Espresso brown cardstock (middle layer, cover art): 5" x 8" (130 x 205mm) rectangle

- Yam orange cardstock (bottom layer, cover art): 5" x 8" (130 x 205mm) rectangle
- Yam orange cardstock (note cards):
  (4) 4" x 6" (100 x 150mm) rectangles

*NOTE CARD DECORATION MADE FROM COVER ART CUTAWAYS

TOOLS AND MATERIALS

- Self-healing cutting mat
- Metal ruler
- Craft knife, such as X-ACTO knife
- Blades for craft knife, such as X-ACTO #11 blades

- 2B pencil
- Adhesive pick-up square
- Liquid adhesive for paper

Note Card Folio Set: Recycling by Design. A photo of a Mandarin duck's streamlined head inspired this sleek motif with a graphic "eye." I cut motifs in a stacked pattern for the decorative folio, then saved the cutaway shapes to decorate the enclosed note cards.

Folio

Mark the folder's cut and score lines.
Trim the cardstock to the specifications shown on the cutting list. Align the butter yellow 10" x 12" (255 x 305mm) sheet on your cutting mat and pencil in lines as shown in the illustration (p. 139). Use solid lines to indicate cut lines and dotted lines to indicate scored lines.

Cut and score the folder to shape.
Cut the solid lines to form the folio's bracing flaps. Score the dotted lines.

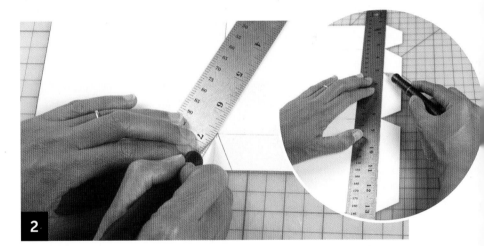

Adhere the bracing flaps. Fold the 5" (130mm)-long top and bottom flaps inward along their score lines, creating sharp creases. Apply glue to the flaps' undersides, making sure to cover the corners. Adhere the flaps to the folder interior and burnish.

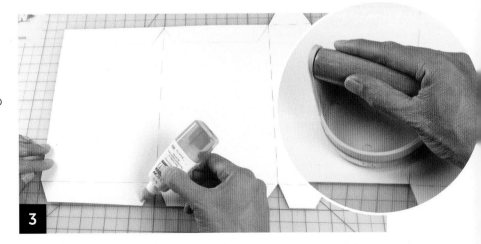

tip: USING TEXTURED CARDSTOCK

If using textured cardstock, the textured side should be the folio's cover; the smooth side forms the folio interior.

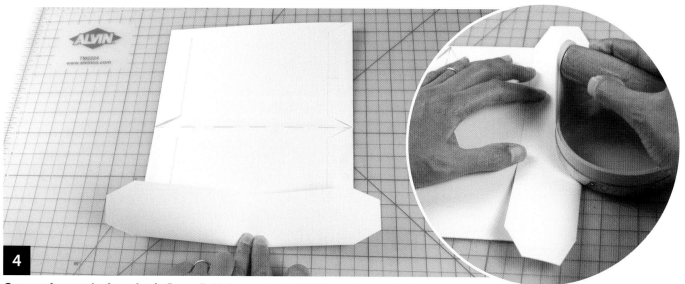

4

Crease the vertical pocket's flaps. Fold the vertical 8" (205mm) scored edge, then crease it sharply. Fold the two 2" (50mm)-long top and bottom flaps inward and crease.

5

Secure the pocket flaps. Leaving the top and bottom flaps folded inward, apply glue to their *top/textured* sides. Flip the entire pocket inward/left along its 8" (205mm) score line and firmly adhere the 2" (50mm) top and bottom flaps to the interior, creating a pocket. You should now have a 5" x 8" (130 x 205mm) pocket folder ready to be decorated with a cover.

Decorative Cover Art

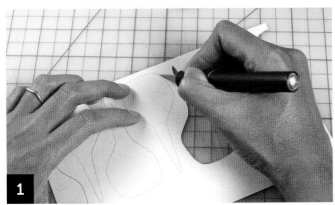

1

Prepare the Duckbill master stencil. Photocopy and transfer the design to the 5" x 8" (130 x 205mm) cardstock. Cut out the shapes and mark this "Master Stencil 1."

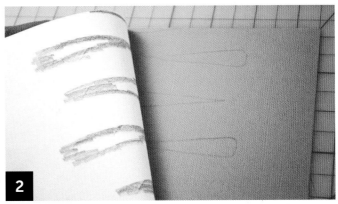

2

Prepare the Teardrop master stencil. Photocopy and transfer the design to a piece of 5" x 8" (130 x 205mm) cardstock. Cut out the shapes and mark this "Master Stencil 2".

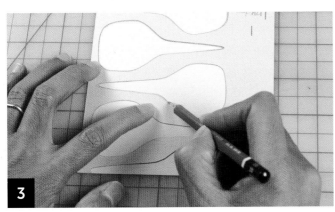

3

Cut the pale blue layer. Align Master Stencil 1 atop the pale blue 5" x 8" (130 x 205mm) layer and draw in the design. Cut out the shapes and set them aside.

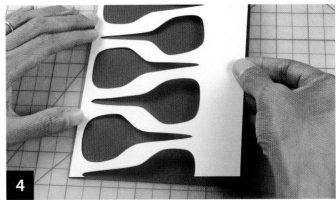

4

Adhere the light blue and brown layers. Apply glue to the back of the pale blue layer. Align the pale blue and dark brown layers, adhere, and burnish. Trim off any overhanging edges.

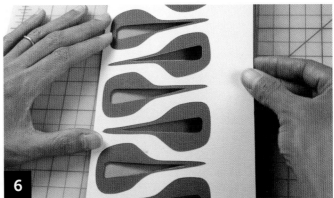

5

Cut the dark brown layer. Align Master Stencil 2 atop the two-ply blue-brown rectangle and lightly draw in the design. Make sure the teardrop shapes rest inside the blue layer's duckbill shapes. Erase and redraw shapes that fell out of registration. Cut out the teardrops and set them aside.

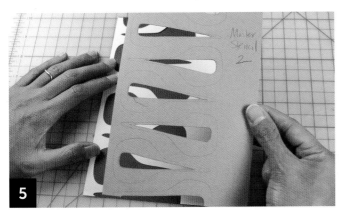

6

Adhere the brown and orange layers. Apply glue to the back of the brown layer. Align it with the orange layer, adhere the layers, and burnish. Trim off any overhanging edges.

Cut the orange layer. Lightly sketch a Duckbill O Shape (see illustration on p. 141) that is ¼" (6mm) high on the orange paper in the widest part of the teardrops. Cut out these shapes and set them aside with the other saved cutaway shapes.

Adhere the artwork to the journal. Place the finished three-ply cover art on the yellow folio's front flap (without the pocket). Be sure the edges of the cover art line up with the folio. Apply glue to the orange layer. Align the corners of the art and the folio, lay together, and burnish. Trim off any overhanging edges. Dab and pull the adhesive pick-up square to remove pencil marks and dried glue on the outside and inside of the folder.

Note Cards

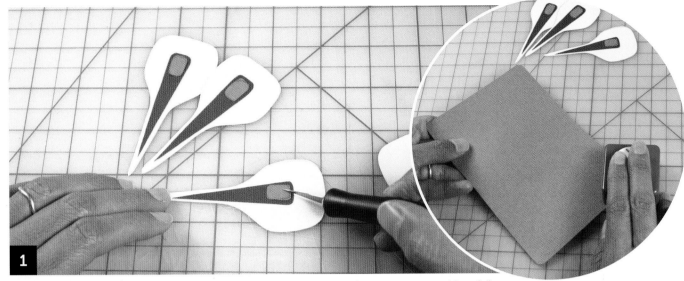

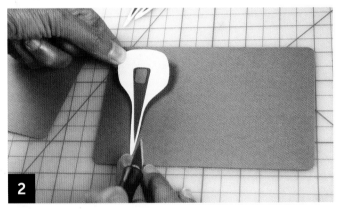

Assemble four recycled duckbill motifs. Gather the cutaway shapes you set aside while creating the Duckbill cover art. Reconstruct four complete duckbills by gluing them in the following order: blue duckbill on bottom, brown teardrop in the middle, and orange O on top. Use a corner punch to round the corners of the 4" x 6" (100 x 150mm) orange cards.

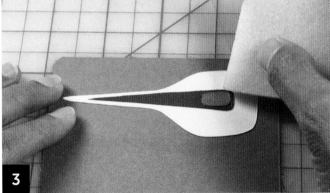

Adhere the artwork to the cards. Glue one duckbill on each of the orange note cards.

Erase pencil marks and assemble the gift set. Remove pencil marks and dried glue with an adhesive pick-up square. Erase in a direction from wider to thinner shapes. Tuck four A6 envelopes and four note cards inside the folder pocket. Burnish one last time, weighting with books to flatten the entire folio. When you present this gift, let your recipient know that the folio folder is frame-worthy!

You Can Also Try:

Making Your Own Envelopes
Paper Source creates a wonderful set of envelope templates (See Resources, p. 142). Use the A6 template, plus the cutting and scoring techniques, to create your own envelopes. Crease them carefully and weight them with books to ensure their flatness.

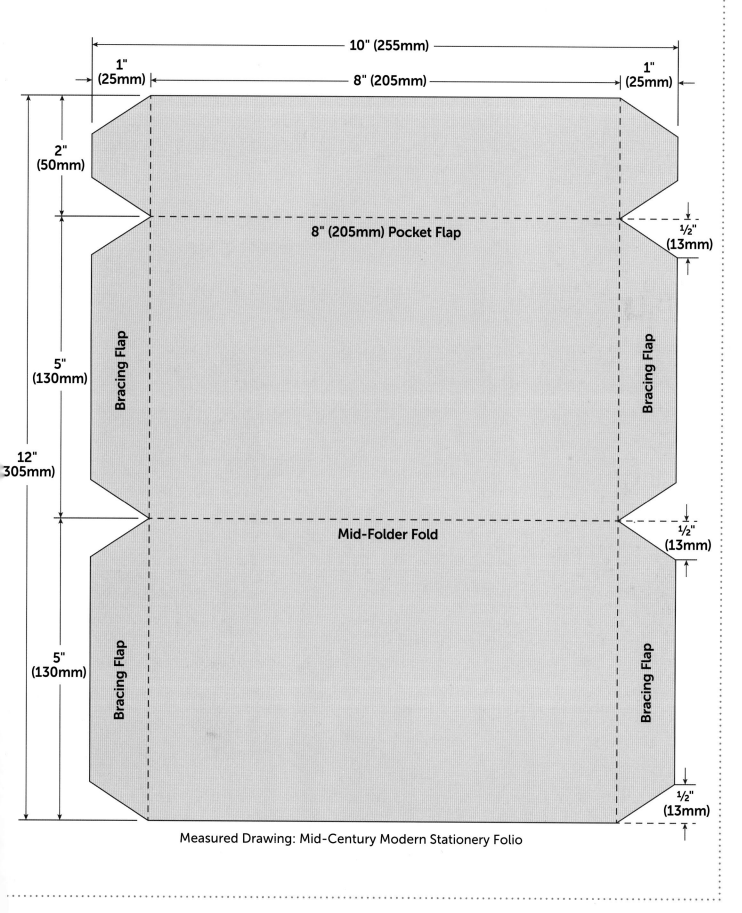

10" (255mm)

1" (25mm)

8" (205mm)

1" (25mm)

2" (50mm)

8" (205mm) Pocket Flap

½" (13mm)

Bracing Flap

5" (130mm)

Bracing Flap

12" (305mm)

½" (13mm)

Mid-Folder Fold

Bracing Flap

5" (130mm)

Bracing Flap

½" (13mm)

Measured Drawing: Mid-Century Modern Stationery Folio

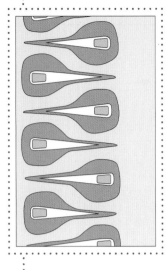

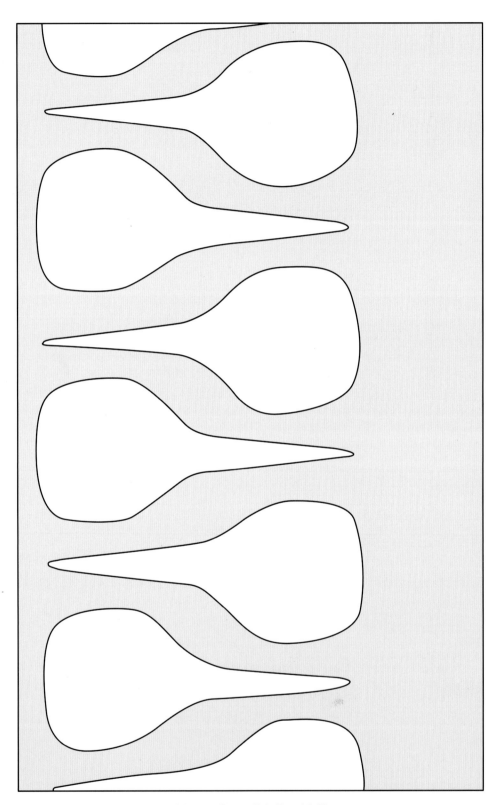

Master Stencil 1: Duckbill

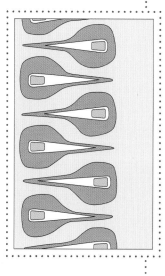

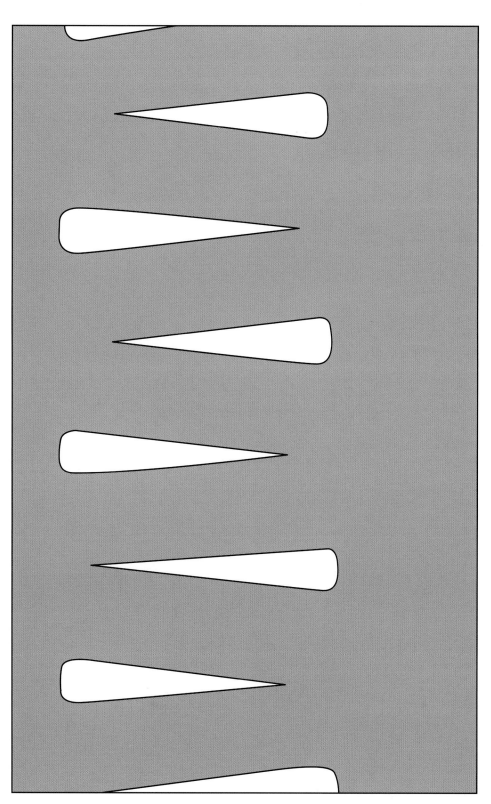

x8

Illustration:
Duckbill "O" Shape

Master Stencil 2: Teardrop

Resources

The author used these products for the projects in this book. Substitute your choice of brands, tools, and materials as desired. Look for these products at your local craft store.

Paper Products

Textured Cardstock
Bazzill Basics Cardstock

Oversized Artist's Cardstock
Canson Mi-Teintes 19" x 25"
(480 x 635mm) cardstock

Envelope Templates
Paper Source

Transfer Paper
Saral Paper

Paper Journals
ReBinder

**Blank Note Cards, Oversized (20" x 26"
[508 x 660mm]) Textured Cardstock**
Strathmore Artist Papers

Adhesive and Sealing Products

Acrylic Spray Sealant
Krylon Paper Finishes Spray Adhesive

Liquid Adhesives for Paper
Tombow USA
Mod Podge Paper (Water-Based Paper Glue
and Sealer)

**Removable Mounting Squares, General-
purpose Spray Adhesive**
3M

Glue Dots
Glue Dots International

**Self-adhesive Easel Backs,
Self-adhesive Book Binder's Tape**
Lineco

Adhesive Pick-Up Squares
Therm O Web
OR
Campbell-Randall

Paper Studio Products

Circular Hand-Held Hole Punch
Fiskars

Professional Combo Circle Template
STAEDTLER Mars

**Self-Healing Cutting Mats,
Cork-Backed Metal Rulers**
Alvin & Company

Craft Knives and Blades
X-ACTO

Printing Barens
Speedball

Corner Rounder, Rotary Paper Cutter
CARL

Artist's Lamp
The Daylight Company LLC

Useful Extras

Resealable Clear Bags
Uline

Ready-Made Wood Frames
ASW

Triptych Frames
IKEA

Three-Ring Recycled Kraft Binder
ACCO Products

Papier Mache Boxes
Darice

Index

Acquisition editor:
Peg Couch

Assistant editors:
Katie Weeber and
Heather Stauffer

Copy editor:
Paul Hambke

Cover designer:
Lindsay Hess

Editor:
Kerri Landis

Layout designer:
Jason Deller

Proofreader:
Lynda Jo Runkle

Indexer:
Jay Kreider

NOTE: PAGE NUMBERS IN *ITALICS* INDICATE PROJECTS.

More Great Books from Design Originals

Stash & Smash
ISBN 978-1-57421-409-3 **$16.99**
DO5380

Pulp Fiction, 2nd Edition
ISBN 978-1-57421-413-0 **$16.99**
DO5384

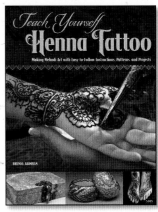

Teach Yourself Henna Tattoo
ISBN 978-1-57421-414-7 **$19.99**
DO5385

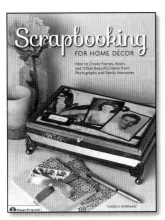

Scrapbooking for Home Décor
ISBN 978-1-57421-411-6 **$19.99**
DO5382

Vision Box Idea Book
ISBN 978-1-57421-407-9 **$16.99**
DO5378

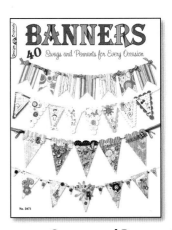

Banners, Swags and Pennants for Every Occasion
ISBN 978-1-57421-348-5 **$8.99**
DO3471

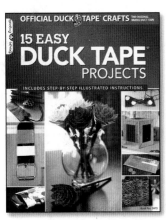

Official Duck Tape® Craft Book
ISBN 978-1-57421-350-8 **$8.99**
DO3473

Steampunk Your Wardrobe
ISBN 978-1-57421-417-8 **$19.99**
DO5388

Zentangle Basics
ISBN 978-1-57421-327-0 **$8.99**
DO3450